Over Where?

…the story of the peregrinations of a peripathetic
GI
who circled the globe in search of a square meal
and a soft bed…

by Sgt Edward Southworth Fisher

Dedicated to the memory of my brother and friend,

George Justus Fisher

PROLOGUE

by Peggy Anne Fisher McNulty, CAPT, Nurse Corps
U.S. Navy Retired

These words were written almost 80 years ago by Dad during WWII at the age of 25. My own Navy career, family and "life" got in the way of my promise to him to get his manuscript published sooner. I re-began this journey after reading a box of hand written letters between my Uncle George serving in the Pacific and my Dad in the years prior to Dad's enlistment. He warned my Dad that if and when he was "called," he should request being assigned anywhere but the infantry and suggested considering the Navy! . After my father's death in 1996, I was privileged to read original letters between him and his family. In letters after the death of my uncle and grandfather, Dad wrote begging my grandmother to allow him to remain overseas and complete his obligation, rather than being transferred home as the sole male survivor in the family. It was a bit like "Saving Private Ryan" in real time.

While reading each page, I learned more of the man we loved for just being my Poppa, exemplary artist, a humble yet ordinary man in most everyone's eyes. I truly experienced his bravery and talent as a writer. I admired his ability to skillfully manipulate the system when he had the opportunity to survive a war that was filled with tragedy and pain.

His story, resembling a true "Mash-like" chain of events, will take you from the small town of Merrick, NY to Africa, China, India, and finally, the Mariana Islands of Saipan and Tinian where the famed "Enola Gay" was launched that ended the war. I laughed and I cried reminiscing this man's enlisted life and escapades in the elite U.S. Army Air Corps.

He magically blends the horrors of the war with his keen wit to unfold a story worth reading and albeit enjoying. He describes this epic war in a unique way that brings the reader closer to him, discovering the fears, limitations, crimes of war and indiscrepancies experienced by this young GI. His friends become your friends; his tragic losses are deeply experienced as your own. His faith seeps through the pages as you become very aware of this young man's morality and goodness.

He is a true hero in my eyes. I regret I wasn't more present in his life to share more of this rich history in person. Life has a way of passing us by too quickly with personal priorities that continually over-ride the importance of this privilege.

I would be remiss not to mention the labors of my beloved "Aunt Ginny," (Dad's sister) in getting this manuscript started. She tirelessly re-typed this entire manuscript before her death, leading the path for completion.

I love you Poppa…You were the one who deserved

the silver eagle that you pinned on my collar, clearly not I!

Fair Winds and Following Seas Shipmate!…

'til we meet again…

CHAPTER 1
IN THE BEGINNING

On the anniversary of the end of "the war to end all wars," Armistice Day, November 11, 1942, I was sworn in to contribute my share to ending the succeeding one. The scene was Grand Central Palace in New York City. We candidates (which, believe it or not, included one blind man and one spastic), clad only in boxer shorts, single-filed our way through a labyrinthine maze of examining rooms at the end of which we received or did not receive the stamp of approval from a bevy of medicos. The chosen ones, me among them, were soon raising our right hands and parroting the oath which put us in Uncle Sam's army.

Two weeks later, along with a group of draftees from my area, I boarded a steam train at Merrick station. Thus, began the metamorphoses meant to change us civilians into spit-and polish soldiers in the short span of six weeks. As the train pulled out of the station and headed east for Yaphank, the Long Island location that had been

1

designated for the start of our transformation, there was promise that the change in us would be rapid indeed, for already there was a crap game in progress on the floor of the train. The click of the galloping dice was loudly accompanied with four-letter references to their difficult combinations.

Yaphank (Camp Upton) was germ city. Everyone coughed and hacked with one communal cold, the contraction of which would prove to become our immunization for the next three years. Inexperienced, and a week later we departed aboard shade-drawn coaches to a "secret" destination, known only to the enemy. Army transportation would prove always to be thus. We soldiers were never entrusted with knowledge of our destination. However, well along on our journey we were informed that we were destined for the fair-haired elitist corps of the army - the high-flying Army Air Corps.

Twenty-four hours later trucks carried us over the

causeway spanning Biscayne Bay to Miami Beach, which was illuminated by an unimaginable full moon. We were billeted in the Indian Queen Hotel, which was to be our hostel during our proposed six-week basic training course. With the exception of a large stain on the ballroom ceiling caused by the overflowing of my room's bathroom sink, little was accomplished in Miami. During our two-week stay the first sergeant seemed to delight in calling us into the street in the middle of the night to stand in ranks for roll call. The last remnants of our communal cold produced a cacophony of backs and coughs from disgruntled GIs who had been deprived of their precious sleep.

Basic training consisted of marching through the streets just after dawn, while singing as we marched. We had strict orders to knock off the singing in the vicinity of the commander's house lest we disturb his beauty sleep. Of course, that's when we sang the loudest. We'd rout step over a footbridge across Indian Creek so that the momentum of our stride didn't shake the bridge to pieces, and come to our destination, a golf course that had been commandeered by the military for an athletic field. This was the scene for calisthenics and other basic nonsense.

After two weeks our basic training was cut short and we entrained and chugged north through the sweltering heat of the day. Night closed about us as we traversed Florida's panhandle. The cold wintery Gulf Coast air infiltrated the unheated coaches through the many open windows, the panes of which had been kicked out by sweating GIs during the heat of the day.

Morning found us in Gulfport, Mississippi, where basic training was to be combined with air-mechanic training. The four-month program would culminate with a week spent on bivouac in a pine woods, a miserable seven days that would teach us just one thing -- the total dysfunction of wet toilet paper.

Our rapid indoctrination into the mores of soldiery

continued at Gulfport. For instance, we learned that the three foremost things on the minds of GIs were sex, food, and sex. A new twist to the vernacular emerged whereby the ever-used four letter words could now be heard inserted between syllables of ordinary words. Also, monthly payday always culminated in an all-night crap game against the latrine wall. Except for one or two fortunates, morning would find all participants penniless. I can still see Whitey with uncensored damnation exhorting his dice to burn on the red-hot cover of the potbellied stove, having sacrificed his entire pay to the god of chance.

Keeping oneself sufficiently fed demanded chicanery and cunning. Surreptitious spiriting of "extras" from the mess-hall under the noses of policing details called for smuggling capabilities that we cultivated with great success. Loaves of bread, jars of jam, oranges, sugar buns were secreted under jackets or passed out windows to be stored on top of the center rafter of our barracks and devoured at subsequent unauthorized feedings. Constant banging of the barracks door caused the jars of jam to slowly walk toward oblivion, and on one occasion the jars hung precipitously over the head of an inspecting officer.

Some friendships were made that lasted throughout the war. Charlie Hess was one of those. It turned out that his father ran a little music store in my old neighborhood in Jamaica that had been frequented by my family. Charlie was an accomplished pianist who played at the Wheatley Hills Tavern in Westbury. Oddly enough, he refused to touch the piano in the day room. He had a heart condition and should never have been in the service. One day I bet him he couldn't chin himself with one hand. He was a tall drink of water and I figured if I couldn't do it, neither could he. He won the dollar. He helped put me together the morning I left for bivouac, my gear shedding from me as I plodded off. I was nursing a hangover that lasted three days. It cured me of over-indulging ever again! The day before had been graduation day from mechanic's school, and I had celebrated my first stripe by trying to drink Biloxi dry. My naivetés gave way to shocked reality when, on my eighth martini, my eyeballs clicked, and I ended up outside throwing up on my shoes.

Every barracks had a cut-up, some overbearing tough guy who found joy in things like turning over cots containing sleeping GIs. Whitey was one of these clowns, and, with his tag along, Moon Mullins, would brag about how they beat up on civilians in the local beer joint on Saturday night. One afternoon the guys were sparring and somehow inveigled me into putting on the gloves. My inexperience was to be pitted against none other than Moon. He was a southpaw and led with his right. When he tried to jab with it, I blocked it with my left and bopped him on the nose with my right. I kept repeating this every time he jabbed and was successful most of the time, although he caught me once with a good one on the nose.

However, he soon got tired of getting bopped and quit. Feeling my oats, I looked at Whitey who had been taking it all in and Said, "How about it, Whitey?" "Naw," he murmured, "I'm too tired."

Whenever we chose up sides and played baseball, Whitey was the slugger, an achievement I envied. One day I was playing centerfield and he was up at bat. When he hit one over my head I ran clear to the shit-house wall to make the best over-the-shoulder one-handed catch that I ever made in my life. Move over, Joe D!

Strange sights in the barracks -- Little Fitzgerald, buff-bare, crouched in the rafters like a monkey, treed by some hazing GIs. The human blowtorch: a fellow who got a charge out of sitting naked in his bunk, igniting his farts with a match. Another who washed his underwear while wearing several sets, one over the other. The routine: soap up in the shower, scrub, peel off one layer at a time, repeat until all were nicely washed and rinsed. Laundry lunatic or not, there really was a method to his madness!

One day in the mess hall, Charlie Hess declared that I was the only person he ever saw who set off sparks with knife and fork! Thus, with sparks flying, I became known as a chowhound. Bourke's wife had come to Mississippi to be with him. They lived off the base. One night he invited me home for a spaghetti dinner. I didn't have a pass, so we slipped through a hole in the fence to avoid the MPs at the gate. I accompanied him home, was introduced to his Italian wife, and nearly killed myself trying to live up to the reputation that had preceded me. Bourke's cry, "Eat, Fisher, Eat!" still rings in my ears!

Charlie's cold still lingered at Gulfport, so his mother sent him a bundle of handkerchiefs. The first week he sent thirty-two soiled ones to the laundry and got back only four. His complaint fell on deaf ears. Their explanation was simple enough...since the official issue was four handkerchiefs, four were all he was entitled.

A good part of our non-school time was spent marching in a column of fours, up and down the company street, learning the intricacies of "to the right march" and "to the rear march," etc. Only one GI out of the entire squadron had been issued a pair of hob-nailed shoes -- Fitzgerald of Glens Falls, New York. He was a slight little guy, ten years or more older than the rest of us. His reflexes had slowed down enough to cause him to be a half step behind the cadence, so that wherever we marched, the click of his heels sounded halfway between our KLUMPS, so it was KLUMP click, KLUMP click, KLUMP click right on down the road.

Breakfast was usually an à la carte affair, consisting of some form of eggs, cereal, toast, juice, coffee, and the ubiquitous beef on toast (a creamy white substance poured over a slice of cardboard) which disliked, if not despised, by 99 out of a 100 GIs. Yet Uncle Sam insisted on serving and garbaging this army UN-delectable which was scornfully referred to as "Shit on a shingle."

There was one GI in the outfit whom we called Duke. He was a lanky, teenage hillbilly from moonshine country, who related a story about how he saw a "mountaineer" shoot down a small plane that some "revenooer" was using to snoop around where some billy had stashed his still. On work detail, Duke would push me aside saying, "Take it easy, Pop" (all 25 years of me), "let me do that."

One day we were marched to the dental clinic where they discovered I had two or three cavities which were promptly filled by a competent buck sergeant dental technician. He then asked me to proceed to the next room where they yanked out a decayed wisdom tooth, completing my entire dental program in one visit.

On a similar occasion my eyes were attended to when another non-com "specialist" performed a quick refraction, unlike those to which I had been accustomed.

He dropped one set of lenses into the contraption mounted on my head, asked how they were, gave them a twist and asked if that was better. I nodded and that was it. Two pairs of glasses in metal frames were issued following his specifications. Surprisingly, they were equal to the civilian pair prescribed after a lengthy examination by an eye specialist involving numerous choices of this lens over that, together with an adjustment for parallax and all that jazz.

About that time a USO entertainment show group came to the base, allowing Gatto from Hoboken to renew his acquaintance with a prostitute who was one of the dancers in the show. Talk about a small world!

Charlie didn't make graduation with me. His schooling had been interrupted when he was issued an emergency pass to visit his sick mother. On get-away day I said good-bye to my best army buddy, and with Fink, from Carle Place, Long Island; and Fitzgerald, from Glens Falls; Gluck, from Lindenhurst; Bourke, from Brooklyn; and the rest of the "shipees," entrained north in coaches of the Illinois Central Railroad.

CHAPTER 2
CHANUTE AND LOWREY FIELDS

Our next "secret" stop was Chanute Field in Illinois, a permanent air force base with many brick buildings, quite unlike our last abode -- a wooden shack in a turpentine plantation in the deep south.. We learned that we were to become "power plant specialists" which would require us to attend engine school for one month.

Aircraft engines are important, in that planes cannot fly without them. The disturbing part was that our skills were to be relied upon to keep those engines running. Although I rated high on the aptitude test given at Upton, in reality, when it came to engines, I wasn't very apt. Suffice it to say, my most trusted job in subsequent years would be draining the sump AFTER the planes had returned from a mission. Be that as it may, I endured school and in due time learned that the re-assembled engine I had completed would not operate without all its parts, particularly without the 18" gear that I had left sitting on the workbench.

Food here was as plentiful as it was unappetizing, but even three squares did not satisfy us. Because Chanute Field had school around the clock, extra feedings were necessary and sometimes *we* were able to take advantage of the situation by partaking of unauthorized servings at odd hours.

It became standard practice, if dessert was good, to go through the mess line one more time, taking a light hit of everything just to get another piece of cake or an extra ice cream. Sad to say some bases discouraged this practice by issuing chow passes, good for only three meals a day.

At the end of each month the order would come for us to fall out in the street in helmet liner and raincoat, sans everything else except shoes. We were then marched in a column of fours, naked as jaybirds underneath our covering, to the infirmary for "short arm" inspection in order to qualify for our monthly pay. Anyone with "syph" or "clapps" was redlined.

Ex-heavyweight champ, Max Baer, and his brother Buddy put in an appearance at the amateur fight arena on the base one evening. Between events they put on a lackluster round of geriatrical fisticuffs. It was obvious they were long out of training. But when those two guys walked into the gym in their long army overcoats, they were so huge they resembled two gigantic haystacks.

A then unknown GI singer by the name of Johnny Desmond entertained in the hall in the evening along with a fabulous jazz trumpeter who was unknown to me, but I'm sure was well known in years to come to jazz aficionados..

Part of the course on engines was devoted to troubleshooting. The instructor would doctor up an engine on the test stand, and then start it up and we were supposed to diagnose the trouble by the sound of the malfunctioning engine. Some guys were good at it, having worked on car engines and such. However, my artist's ears always failed to inform my brain of the necessary information to affect a successful repair. If you stood behind the engine when it was operating properly and running full blast, the test stand vibrated so much it made your teeth ache, while the prop wash popped your eyeballs.

Late summer arrived, and with-it completion of the course and an added stripe. Then shipment. We packed our duffle bags and fell out into the street at 8 AM to wait for the trucks to arrive. With the usual delay, they didn't pick us up until 2 PM to drive us to the train. By now we were long used to the daily roll call that ran from "A" through names like Bialostoski (whom they re-named Murphy), Fink, Fisher, Fitzgerald, Gluck, ad infinitum. However, on this day, when the roll reached Fink, the roll call ceased and Fisher, Fitzgerald and Gluck remained standing on the platform as super-numeraries -- replacements for anyone indisposed.

Since no replacements were needed, we were told to report back to our orderly room and then to await further orders. Good soldiers that we were, we did just that and thus became lost to all authority for one solid month before a bed-check unfortunately revealed our existence. Our vacation from all duties was abruptly terminated. We had thoroughly enjoyed four weeks of: up at 10, meals at any of the multiple feedings, snooker in the afternoon, then a dip in the pool followed by a movie in the evening, ice cream at the PX, cards or whatever else until we felt like flopping into our bunks where we were left undisturbed until we decided to rise and do it all over again. There was just one drawback. In order to avoid bringing attention to ourselves, we had to forego applying for a weekly pass to Chicago.

Two days after we were finally discovered, we shipped out with the next group of graduates on another "secret" train ride to Lowrey Field in Denver, where a third school awaited our attendance. We were now to become "armament specialists." The course took one month to complete during which time the only acquired skill was the breaking down and reassembling of a caliber 50 machine gun while blindfolded. This skill I was never again called upon to perform. I qualified as marksman with the colt 45, but failed to qualify with the springfield, which kicked like a mule and wouldn't even hit the target, even though (in disbelief) I called for a re-score (like sergeant York, aka Gary Cooper).

Off days were spent hitchhiking to Golden, and even to Cheyenne, Wyoming, 90 miles to the north. Fink, Fitzgerald, Gluck, and I rented a car and drove to Buffalo Bill's grave atop Lookout Mountain.

The weird story of your "feet's too big" starts at Chanute Field where I put a pair of shoes in for repair but shipped out before they were ready. I was forced to take a wrong size replacement until such time as an exchange could be made at my next base. Accordingly, at Lowrey, I tried to make the swap but to no avail. Believe it or not, no change in shoe size could be made without permission from a doctor, so the next morning I had to go on sick call, wait for the bus to the hospital, shoes in hand, and spend a red-tape morning obtaining a medical OK for a size 11 pair of shoes!

To avoid the daily calisthenics requirement at Lowrey, Roy White, our barracks leader devised a plan whereby we were allowed to play baseball instead. Every afternoon Roy would dutifully check out bats and gloves, then hide them under his bunk so that "the team" could take off, each man on his own. Along about the fourth week, however, we struck out enmasse. Word came down that baseball was cancelled for the day.

Instead we were marched to the parade grounds where "our team" was positioned along the perimeter of the great square field which was entirely checkerboarded with individual formations from every barracks on the base. We were to perform in a mass calisthenic review. White made a final appeal to be spared from this ordeal to no avail. He returned to our group and whispered, "Every man for himself!" Our formation disintegrated and in moments we were gone with the wind.

Our tyrannical leader, Captain Tassitano, was a native of Brooklyn, and a veteran, as he put it, of the Pineapple Squad. He saluted with his left hand, his motionless gloved right hand hanging useless at his side. "You can call me a one-armed son of a bitch," he would say, "but not to my face!" His favorite form of punishment was to have any miscreant dig a hole 6'x 6' x 6', upon completion of which he would toss a cigarette butt into the hole and order the digger to fill it up. He wasn't all "bite," however. He once allowed some of us to escape punishment when we were caught in the barracks during baseball time.

About this time Roy White found himself in a predicament. It seems he was playing around with a girl in town, when out of the blue his wife decided to come to Denver for a share of his affection. I guess one could say that Roy suffered from too much of a good thing!

KP was probably the worst torture that the average GI endured. From 4 AM to 6 PM he was forced to subject himself to the abuse of the KP pusher. The latter's sole duty was to make life miserable for the lowly GI who had been singled out by fate to administer sustenance to his fellow GIs. It was "go-go-go" with hardly a letup. During the occasional respite from the arduous tasks of the day, one might grab forty winks stretched out on a table or under a sink. At least one could scrounge for food, as I did on one occasion. I managed to secrete a whole cherry pie which I proceeded to nibble on when the coast was clear. Alas, three quarters of the way through my luscious booty, I was collared by the dreaded KP pusher, who shoved a mop into my hand and led me to the site of my punishment, a large room that he ordered me to swab. Around the four walls of that room were tiers of shelves and upon each shelf were rows of freshly baked pies! Here in Pie Heaven, I didn't whistle while I worked, but I sure did nibble!

One stint of KP had us scrubbing down tables and floors, wringing out dirty mops, etc., at the end of which we were ordered to cut bread for lunch. Blackened hands grabbed loaves and sliced a mountain of bread, leaving black smudges all over those lily-white slices. They were served later in the chow line, with orders to handle the slices with forks to avoid contamination of the bread, of course!

Latrine duty was usually reserved for the foul-ups, and often was assigned permanently to the most ill-fit GI. Toilets were aligned the length of the latrine with no enclosures so that privacy was non-existent. One base actually had a sign over the end toilet in the row designating it for venereal disease only! I never saw anyone sitting on it. It was probably the safest seat in town.

Fall found us one stripe richer and on our way to the next "secret" base. We entrained as far as Wichita and lay over for the night. This enabled us to visit town and take in a movie and vaudeville featuring Count Basie with Cosey Cole on drums. Next day, our cars were hooked up to a freight train and we traveled west on a one-track railroad across the plains of Kansas toward our "secret" destination. We pulled into one small town consisting of one street that stretched out from the tracks. Since some of our accompanying freight cars had to be dropped at a siding, we had several minutes to visit town. When the engineer had finished shunting cars, a prearranged signal would call us back to the train. All too soon blasts from the locomotive's whistle sounded and GIS streamed back from town laden with food and beer (3.2, since no liquor could be purchased in Kansas without a doctor's prescription, which had to be filled at a drugstore). As luck would have it, Dougherty even got to visit one of his four ex-wives who happened to reside in town! Later on, he distinguished himself and won the soldier's medal for snuffing out a gasoline fire on the wing of a B-29 with his bare hands.

Our "secret" destination proved to be Pratt, Kansas, the asshole of the world, but upon arrival we were turned away, evidently unworthy of such a lowly station. They placed us in a convoy and transported us by road to Salina where again we unwelcomed. From there we were sent to what would be our station for the next six months.

CHAPTER 3
ON THE LINE

We arrived at Smokey Hill Air Force Base near Great Bend, Kansas and were assigned to the 444th Bomb Group (heavy) of the 58th Wing. The group consisted of four squadrons -- the 676th, 677th, 678th and 679th. Fitz and Gluck went into the 678th, and I was put into the 679th. Each squadron boasted one airplane -- a B-29 Superfortress, the latest U.S. bomber, bigger, better, and faster than any plane ever built. Its payload was ten tons of bombs. Its speed was redlined at 350 MPH.

We settled down to the humdrum existence of working on the line, alternating weekly between day and night twelve-hour shifts. Word came down one day that we were to be considered for aircraft gunners. This entailed taking a physical during which a question arose about my ability to see certain colors, as certain numbers were invisible to me on the test cards. Red and green color blindness was suspected so I was ushered before the presiding officer to be examined further. He dumped a pile of yarn fragments on the table, picked up a piece of blue-green yarn and asked me to match it from the pile. I searched but couldn't find one of the exact color. When I mentioned that there was no other green that shade, he told me to pick any green and red, which I was very able to do. The physical now completed, a reviewing officer took over. He read the results of my test and then asked, "soldier, would you want to be a gunner?" Consent was necessary, for they could not make you fly. With a burst of patriotism, I blurted, "Yes, sir." He replied, "sorry, you can't fly with glasses." You may well ask, why did they bother to give me a physical in the first place. The follow up to this story is that one month later the line chief approached me with the information that they were now accepting gunners with glasses. Did I want to reapply? I shook my head. After all, I'd broken my record of never volunteering for anything in the army and I wasn't foolish enough to break it again.

The line chief called me in one day and asked me if I would paint a pinup girl on the nose of our B-29. Information in my service record had tipped him off to my profession, and it took some convincing to make him understand that making mechanicals in a studio did not qualify me for billboard painting. Next thing I knew, Squires was struggling to do a six-foot pinup on a metal plane using pastels! He later switched to paint, and his sign-painting skills helped him to become a pretty good pinup artist. Once overseas his talent was in great demand to produce raunchy bits of pulchritudinous nudity on the sides of Uncle Sam's aircraft. And so, I missed my chance to become the Peter Arno of the U.S. Army Air Force.

As fall slipped into winter, we were surrounded with brown corn-stubble fields stretching to the horizon. Small islands of trees, mere clumps surrounding occasional farmhouses, were the only relief offered upon the bleak pancake terrain of Kansas. Winter snow and sub-freezing temperatures were ours to endure.

In December I exceeded the ten-mile limit on my two-day pass by taking a bus ten miles north of Great Bend to Hoisington, a whistle-stop on The Union Pacific Railroad, where I caught the streamliner for Kansas City, Missouri, two hundred miles away. For one glorious day in a real city I Christmas shopped and whiled away some time at the Nelson Art Museum. Enroute to Hoisington that night, I was picked up by two MPs who were checking GI passengers. But since I was on my way back to camp, they let me go. Arriving in Hoisington at 3 AM, I set out on foot along the dark road to Great Bend, ten miles away. There was no moon, no streetlights, and the wintry wind whistled through the electric wires strung on poles along the side of the road. The occasional barking of a dog indicated the presence of some habitation although none was visible. Several cars failed to heed my thumb until one stopped after I'd walked about three miles. The car was filled with drunk guys and gals, so I declined their invitation to squeeze in. Several miles later a gentleman stopped and brought me into Great Bend as dawn was breaking. After grabbing a bite at the cockroach diner, I caught the bus back to base in time for roll call.

Guard duty was brutal in winter. I pulled twenty-four-hour duty (2 on, 4 off) following a blizzard that left us in sub-zero weather that a fleece-lined coat, pants, shoes, and hat could not repel. To keep from freezing, I was forced to jump up and down, standing on the seat of the guard house from 2 to 4 AM.

At Great Bend I became buddies with Jim Murphy from Bogota, New Jersey, and Bill Lee from Washington, D.C. by way of China. Lee was a Chinese laundryman before joining the service. He spoke little English, but his speech improved rapidly. He told me about shirt ironing, Chinese style, using a pair of irons that were warmed on a stove. Each iron had enough heat retention to iron one shirt, so that a rhythm of one iron, one shirt was maintained through the pressing procedure. However, one of his customers was a very big individual, and the iron would cool off before one of his shirts was completely ironed. Regardless, Lee would stick to his normal routine with the result that the big man's shirt suffered, and he started to complain about poor workmanship and finally took his shirts elsewhere. A short time later, he came back, for no other Chinese laundry would service him. Little did he know that the Chinese characters of identification that Lee had inked inside the collar of his shirts spelled out "tough man." The old saying, "no tickee, no shirtee" was indeed true, as Lee explained it to me. Even when he knew who owned a particular shirt, he would not relinquish it without a ticket. Ah, the ways of the wily Oriental!

A ten-day pass issued before Christmas allowed me my only furlough home, and it was good to see my family again. Although it's hard to believe, after a week I was anxious to get back to Great Bend. I guess I was just not used to the contrast of life at home. I would actually lie in bed at night and try to picture another bed two feet above me. One of the GI expressions of the day was, "you've found a home in the army." I hate to think that this was true, but one must realize that the war was far from being over and our new way of life would be a long-term reality.

Some of the lessons that were learned at Gulfport were put to good use, especially on night shift. For instance, after our breakfast was served at midnight, we'd exit the mess hall through the kitchen, passing the room where large sheet cakes rested awaiting the next day's serving. It was so simple to slip inside and steal a huge wedge to sustain me until the 6 AM second breakfast, that you might call it "a piece of cake."

We got a chance to shoot skeets once, and I knocked down half of the twenty birds from the different positions stationed around the high and low houses from which the birds were launched, one at a time. But when we shot doubles, two at a time, a "hot shot" I was not -- in fact, I did poorly.

The group was reorganized into three squadrons, mine being eliminated. I was transferred to the 676th along with Murphy and Lee. Shortly thereafter, we were placed aboard a train heading for another "secret" destination, traveling eastward to St. Louis, and then southeast through the beautiful Kanawa River Valley of West Virginia, past Charleston, home of Roy White, to Norfolk, Virginia, the embarkation port for overseas.

An entire new series of shots was given to us to immunize us against smallpox, cholera, typhus, typhoid, yellow fever, and the black plague. Occasionally the prevention became the killer. The previous time we were given cholera shots, one unfortunate buddy of mine died from an asthma attack, aggravated by the shot. After that incident, asthmatics were exempted from receiving them. We fired Springfields again, this time on a pistol range, two guys sharing a rifle, one to coach the other as he fired. Our rifle had a hair trigger, the least pressure causing it to fire. While my buddy was firing, the cease-fire order came. I tapped him on the shoulder as he raised his weapon causing it to discharge a shot into the ceiling. It drew a little attention. We were issued carbines, a comfortable little semi-automatic rifle that we tested on a pistol range. My forty shots chopped a two-inch hole in the target slightly down and to the right of the bull's eye. From then on I was able to compensate for the nonadjustable sight when I used the gun later on -- not to kill the enemy, but to plink bobbing beer bottles!

CHAPTER 4
OVERSEAS

On Lincoln's birthday, February 12, 1944, we embarked on a "secret" voyage aboard the Liberty ship Joseph Hollister, sailing from Hampton Roads. Five hundred of us were billeted in the 'tween decks in racks of five. These were slung from the ceiling and surrounded a makeshift wooden dining area over the central hatch cover which concealed the cargo below. Each bunk was approximately twenty-four inches wide and seven feet long with a clearance of two feet between bunks.

Inside this area, so cramped that when you rolled over your knees would hit the rump of the guy above, you had to stow all your gear: helmet, rifle, gas mask, musette bag, barracks bag, duffle bag, belt with knife and canteen, an extra pair of shoes and your mess kit. Of course, the bags contained an overcoat, winter OD jacket with two pairs of wool pants, two sets of sun-tans, your other set of fatigues, a flight jacket, winter and summer underwear (two sets), four pairs of socks, three or four caps, four handkerchiefs, shaving gear and any other personal stuff you wanted to carry. Needless to say, I slept with my clothes on, even right on down to my shoes. After six days it was evident that athletes' feet reveled in these conditions, and I was forced to remove my shoes and scratch. What the hell, I even took a shower! One reason I was reluctant to undress was that I wanted to be ready to abandon that old tub on the double should we be torpedoed. What bothered me most was the hole in one of the two tubes encircling my waist that were supposed to keep me afloat if we went over the side.

To digress. We sailed to join a convoy off the coast, and on the second day, eighty ships were stretched across the ocean to the horizon. Our ship was toward the rear in the next to last of ten or twelve rows, so that to our left steamed the bulk of the convoy. What a beautiful sight it was to see such a mass of ships steaming along together, a large white yacht leading the parade, while corvettes circled the convoy for its protection. We proceeded to the "destination unknown" at a slow six to seven knots.

Most of us got our sea legs early, although the small ship had movement, and almost all of us had steady stomachs after the first day; Dixon was the exception. He already had his head in the toilet before we got out of the harbor.

On the third evening we sailed into a maelstrom. The ship started to toss and so did many stomachs. All during the night the storm raged outside. Some of the ocean occasionally poured down the ladders into our hold. The lantern hanging from the ceiling swung to an angle of forty degrees. The jerry-built dining room collapsed in a pile of kindling that slid back and forth over the hatch cover all night. Fifty-gallon drums broke loose and rumbled back and forth overhead. At least half of the GIs were throwing up. One of those poor unfortunates was seen crawling along the tilting floor heaving into his upturned helmet as he went. I held on to the frame of my bunk lest I be catapulted to the floor below and tried to cat nap between rolls of the ship, instinctively tightening my grip at the height of each roll. Otherwise, I felt fine.

By morning things had quieted down considerably and we were allowed topside. I glanced across the giant waves as our ship tossed and rolled and saw nothing but water -- not one single ship of the convoy could be seen. We were alone. Our port lifeboat had been swept away from its davits on the bridge deck and a landing barge strapped to the rear deck had shifted precariously but held. The Atlantic was still tossing up thirty-foot waves, one of which slapped the side and wet me down good. Slowly, ships began to appear on the horizon and by nightfall the entire convoy had reassembled, continuing its voyage to where?

Days were spent either lying on the main deck hatch

cover watching the mast slowly tilt with each twenty-degree roll, playing cards, or reading in the shirt-sleeve weather that prevailed. Dixon remained in the head, urping one minute and regaling fellow head visitors the next with a tongue that never ceased to flap with its southern cadence. For one reason or another his mouth was open for the entire day. And it was thus for the entire voyage.

During the nights, the convoy was blacked out. There was no moon overhead when we stood the submarine watch. We were led from within the lighted ship through a maze of blackout curtains to the deck outside where it was so dark we could see absolutely nothing for several minutes. I don't know how the fellow leading us was able to take us to our post. Once stationed, we would stand staring out across what could faintly be recognized as the swell of the ocean, by the light of the stars alone. No one told us what we were supposed to do on the slim chance that we could make anything out, but it did give me a spooky part to play in our little game of war.

One afternoon they uncovered the five-inch gun on the foredeck, released a balloon and waited for it to reach a high altitude. They then proceeded to try and knock it out with explosive shells, one of which exploded close enough to the balloon to be cheered by all. I was standing next to Krupa, one of our aircraft gunners. As we watched the black puffs of smoke from the bursting attack, he murmured to me, "Boy, that's what scares me the most, getting shot down by that stuff."

One sunny morning the powers-that-be called for a crab inspection, not unlike the ritual performed before payday each month, to prove oneself free of venereal disease and eligible to receive one's monthly stipend. The inspection was held in the 'tween decks, the doc sitting on a chair searching for vermin as the GIs filed by, their private jewels exposed to his scrutiny. During this grand parade someone above, who was sliding the heavy wooden covers of the hatch in an attempt to open it, inadvertently let one slip. The heavy cover crashed into the hold, delivering a glancing blow to the head of the medic, cold conking him in the process.

Smiles aside, it was a tragedy for the concussion was serious and there was no one to treat him. Next day a corvette pulled alongside our ship and fired a line aboard, rigged a breeches buoy and managed to get the doctor aboard in spite of a dunking he received when the line slackened as the two ships bobbed and twisted in the rough seas. I could see right under the corvette's brow every time it pitched out of the sea. The next morning, we were kept below while they transferred the patient to the corvette. Word had it that the medic had lost his sight.

One evening, we were treated with a makeshift amateur hour hosted by the chaplain. Entertainment consisted of such mediocre renditions as Connor's nasal warbling of the Wabash Cannonball, and Wyzola's mellifluous tootling on the ocarina, after which the padre discreetly retired from the premises to let boys be boys and jokes be dirty.

The ship's original tiny head (toilet) was augmented with a very dimly lit shelter on the aft deck containing a long open trough over which was mounted a row of twenty toilet seats. Sea water constantly flushed the trough in a steady stream that entered at one end and bubbled fluorescently in the semi-dark on its passage under the seats to exit out the other end. In theory this simple arrangement seemed adequate to the task it was expected to perform. However, it must have been designed by a landlubber who had reckoned with only one movement! Aside from the human function, there was also the movement of the ship to consider. If one didn't raise and lower one's functioning parts in rhythm with the motion of the ship, the inevitable backwash would cause a reactionary movement as the flow reversed itself and rushed back up the trough. Heady stuff,

I assure you! Excuse me for wondering, but would a chorus of "I've Got Rhythm" be in order?

On the twentieth day we sighted land and the convoy split up. The Hollister headed through the Straits of Gibraltar into the blue waters of the Mediterranean and proceeded between Spain and Morocco along the north coast of Africa to what turned out to be our objective, the Port of Oran in Algeria.

At the entrance of the harbor an armada of dories surrounded the ship. They were loaded with souvenirs, all available at prices determined through the shouted deliberations of the merchants and purchasers. Lines had been thrown aboard with baskets attached so that the prospective buyer could haul up the articles for inspection and, should a price be agreed upon, the buyer would accede to the command of the seller to send the money by placing it in the basket for the return trip to the dory below.

The Hollister docked at a quay in the small harbor

below the town. At chow time, and even as we lined up on

deck, mess kits in hand, waiting to be served, trucks pulled

alongside. The order came to disembark, as there would be

"a hot meal at the staging area." Thereupon 500 men left

500 hot meals in the galley: 1,000 pork chops, 150 pounds

of mashed potatoes, a steamer full of string beans, and a vat

of chocolate pudding-- all this to feed three GIs who had

been left behind to clean up the ship. I was one of those lucky three. I guess you might call it a dream come true! Although we did the very best we could, somehow we couldn't quite finish it all. The leftovers were jettisoned. The next day our Captain came back to the ship to beg the ship's Captain for some food. He got a ham for his trouble (for the officer's mess, of course). The hot meal promised the 500 men turned out to be cold "C" rations. Our Captain advised us to steal what food we could, as the GIs were starving. Before we left the ship the following day, I had garnered all that I could scrounge -three pounds of cocoa, several cans of evaporated milk, sugar, crackers, and a gallon can of something without a label.

While aboard we had time to watch the Algerian stevedores. They all wore pantaloons that resembled diapers, oddly paired with western style jackets. Their task was to unload the ship's cavernous hold, which was one gigantic compartment chock full of crates and bundles in a solid mass that filled it wall to wall, from deck to keel.

Trucks took us up the winding road from the dock to the town of Oran situated on the top of a plateau. We drove through the town eastward to a tent camp several miles away. We were issued three extra blankets each, although it was 70 degrees outside. It wasn't long before we discovered why. After sundown, the temperature quickly plummeted to freezing, with the cold so penetrating that five blankets and all our clothes, including overcoat, gloves, and hat, could not keep us warm. During the five days we were there, we brewed hot cocoa every night and shared what we had with our tent buddies. It helped to fill the void left by the inadequacy of cold "C" rations.

At Oran, a standing order existed to the effect that all transients must take one ten-mile hike with a full pack. Thankfully, our commanding officer successfully interceded with the base commander to spare the Air Corps from the embarrassment of trying to perform an ordeal more suited to the infantry.

On getaway day, while sitting on all our gear in the company street waiting for the trucks which would take us to our next unknown destination, we decided to share the only food left in our larder -- the mystery giant gallon can. My trench knife cut into the lid, as our little group anxiously awaited, hoping against hope that it wasn't sauerkraut, ketchup, or piccalilli. For once we lucked out -- it turned out to be applesauce. Applesauce might not rate high on your list of gourmet preferences, but under present circumstances it hit a stupendous nine!

We trucked back to the dock and were put aboard the Champolion, an old-style cruise ship with a castle amid ship, a low deck fore and aft of it, and a forecastle and high poop deck at the bow and stern, respectively. An extra gun deck had been added over the poop, which tended to rattle when we were underway. On the top of the main castle, next to the stack, rocket-launchers were mounted. The crew was French, but the troop command was British so that we came under the supervision of a Colonel from a Scottish Regiment, complete with trews (tartan trousers), a tam-o-shanter and a swagger stick. He was a spit-and-polish man of the old school who just did not comprehend such a slovenly group of ill-fitted GIs like us.

The Champolion proceeded eastward through the blue waters of the Mediterranean as all hands were called to assemble on the main deck for inspection by the British Colonel. We had convinced Dixon, who was already confined below with mal de mer, to give it a try on deck, as the sea was as calm as glass. He made it topside, stood for a brief moment, then ran for the rail. The Brit called us to attention, and it immediately must have become apparent to his narrow military mind that the soldiers who stood before him in disarray were a sorry ragtag lot who would present nothing but problems in the days ahead.

There were no bunks aboard. Each evening we

chose either a mattress or a hammock which we could hang or flop anywhere we chose. I opted for the mattress, but eventually found it more pleasant to flop on the steel deck, my shoes tucked beneath my head for a pillow, with a sky full of stars for a blanket. Mornings would find me surrounded and covered with ash that had belched out of the funnel all night.

There was a dining area in one large cabin where tasteless British fare was served three times a day. Anyone who enjoyed a breakfast of stewed tomatoes, and coffee that tasted like tea should not qualify as a member of the human race. I never gave our GI cooks a "chef" rating, but compared to the British, I would give them at least an "Oscar" (of the Waldorf, of course!). The food was tasteless and inadequate and much of what they served went out the porthole together with what they called dessert -- a soggy loaf of bread covered with a thick shellac-like sauce not fit for the sharks.

We skirted the North African coast until we arrived off Cape Blanc, at which point we turned north-eastward. As we turned, one seaman was observed paying off a bet with his companion. Apparently even the French crew was unsure of our route, but now it became evident that we were to sail across the Tyrrhenian Sea. We passed under the cliffs of Capri and entered Naples harbor, tying up at a mole in the outer harbor, warped there by a flat-decked decadent tug with no wheelhouse. Steering the tug was a voluble Napolitano who argued across the water with the pilot about the best way to put us in. Adjacent Vesuvius vented vapors skyward as we settled down for the night.

Noises awakened me during the night as I slept below decks, and taking them to be made by the ship scraping the dock, I promptly went back to sleep only to learn the next morning that the German Air Force had dropped some calling cards in an attempt to make Naples our final destination. Glass was shattered on the bridge and fish floated in the harbor, seemingly the lone victims of the recent Nazi bombing.

All the next day we lay in the harbor, listening to the guns of the front lines some sixty miles north of us, somewhere below Rome. Evening brought with it a drenching downpour which lasted all night, presumably preventing Jerry from dropping more eggs on us. The morning light revealed a smoking Vesuvius, its upper half covered with snow. At dusk we put out to sea. Outside the harbor a British destroyer laid down a smoke screen around us as we steamed southeastward to pass through the Straits of Messina the following morning. The ship's radio picked up a German broadcast claiming they had sunk a B-29 outfit in Naples harbor. Could it have been loose lips in Oran that tipped off the Krauts?

We rounded the toe of Italy up three ships and a Brit destroyer escort and sailed eastward to parts unknown, passing a floating mine-a-bristle with protruding detonators close to our port side. No effort was made to detonate it as it floated astern, perhaps to strike some unwary vessel later on. However, later in the voyage one salvo of rockets was fired in the air just for the hell of it.

The Brits were opportunists of the first order. When we helped load supplies at Oran before sailing, I could see the Brit supply sergeant's eyes light up at the sight of American sugar -- not in 100 lb. sacks but packaged in convenient five pound sacks, perfect for exchange for the favors of the female persuasion. American PX supplies were also put aboard, for our convenience, of course, but promptly went on sale in the Brit store at their convenient, highly inflated prices.

Naturally, the Brit Commander attempted to make the lot of the GI more difficult by staging daily calisthenics. Putting the brain cells to work, I soon devised a devious way to avoid this displeasure. By positioning myself in the rear of the adjoining group, I could turn to face the group that was resting while the other group was busy performing all those uncomfortable gyrations.

Several days cruising brought us off the coast of Alexandria, then to Port Said, at the head of the Suez Canal. It became obvious that our destination lay somewhere beyond, for the next day we sailed into that man-made waterway to proceed southward toward the Red Sea. The dory belonging to a souvenir wallah had been hoisted aboard and placed on the forward deck. During the entire passage through the canal, the proprietor was able to sell enough souvenirs to put a large dent in our supply of pocket money -- a lucrative arrangement indeed, both for the wallah and for the ship's captain.

Our vocabulary was improved somewhat with the addition of a few words from the vernacular of the area, one being "hubba," an exclamation of appreciation, particularly of womankind. Another was "bok-sheesh," meaning tip, alms, any freebie, a constant request after a service was rendered, or for no service at all.

We proceeded through the "big ditch" with sand and desert, flanking both sides with guns situated at regular intervals. Only one in ten were manned with real artillery, the rest sported only wooden fakes. Traffic moved in one direction only. By the afternoon we had passed the town of Suez and filed into Great Bitter Lake, there to pass the night waiting for the north-bound traffic to clear from the lower canal. Next morning, we proceeded southward through the lower canal and entered the Red Sea at the foot of Mount Sinai, only to discover that the Red Sea is really green.

By now the food had become intolerable. Bread put aboard at Said was like powdered concrete and was tossed out the portholes into the sea along with the other inedibles served to us by our British cousins. One afternoon GIs put on a demonstration that rivaled scenes from "The Big House," where convicts pounded their metal cups on the

54

dining room tables and shouted in unison, "We were served rancid meat." We, too, pounded our tables with our mess-kit cups and shouted in unison, "Some shit! Some shit!" This cacophony aroused the Brit Commander, who came down to inquire about the din. He refused to follow our suggestion that he taste the meat and beat a hasty retreat. Next day we were served American "C" rations, not gourmet fare, but an unbelievably welcome substitute for the limey diet. On succeeding days, "C" rations continued to be interspersed with Brit-shit until the end of the voyage.

During the latter stages of the trip, our American Commander, whom we never saw, over-imbibed and fell down a flight of stairs. He was replaced at our next station.

We sailed past Jiddah, seaport for the holy city of Mecca in Saudi Arabia, and then on to the end of the Red Sea and through the Strait of Bab el Mandeb. Rounding the tip of Arabia, we put in at the then British port of Aden, a coaling station on the Arabian Sea. From Aden, it was a straight run eastward to Bombay, India. Before disembarking we were given another smallpox vaccination, since they had misplaced our shot records. This made the third time in a year that I was immunized, a misnomer indeed since none of them took. (Note: The Champolion served out the war only to come to grief while ferrying Israeli refugees from Europe several years later. It sank off the coast of Israel in a storm). After disembarking we were put on a train with two cases of "K" rations to a car, and were taken to a British camp, guarded by Gurkhas, and billeted with Sikh troops.

There were also British soldiers and a bunch of Italian prisoners of war, captured by the Brits in North Africa. When we left the train, I noticed an unopened case of rations, and presuming we would have need of it, I carried it off the train. We broke it up in the street and divided the spoils. They proved to be lifesavers, for the food was so bad at the camp that we were fortunate to be able to augment our diet with the "Ks" which were pretty good. Each package contained a can of ham and eggs or chicken or beef, crackers, a candy bar, chewing gum, cigarettes, matches and toilet paper.

The latter most appropriately was the official GI color tan.

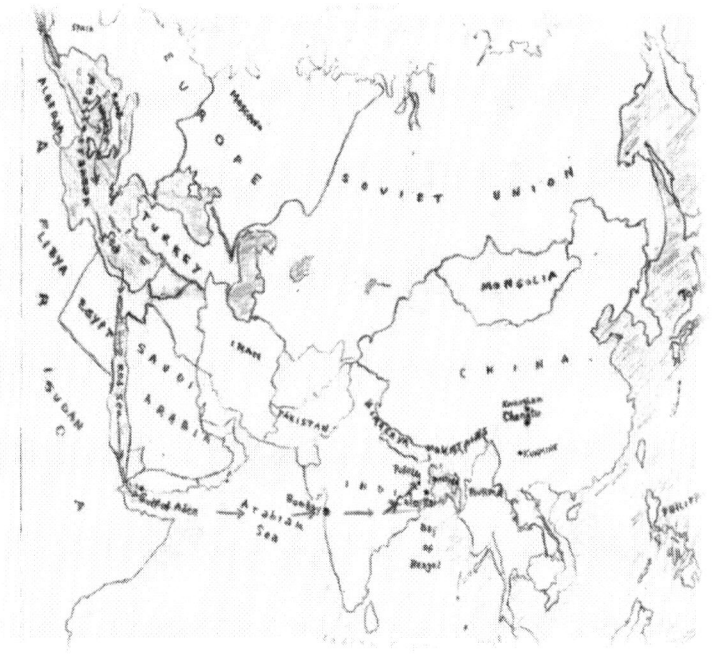

The British chow was prepared by native cooks in an open-air kitchen under a canopy of flies that swarmed over everything. It looked worse than it tasted, which wasn't good, but the hawks didn't mind. As we ate, they flew in over our shoulders and snatched the meat from our mess kits.

We lived in tents made with two layers of canvas, with six inches of airspace in between. This helped to insulate us from our tropical environment. Every afternoon, the tea-wallah would canvas the aisles between the tents, offering hot tea, which seemed to be the drink of India despite the heat. For half a rupee he would fill your mess cup and for another equal payment, you could purchase a large cookie. It wasn't long before he was hawking his wares in a strange way. Some wiseacre GI had once facetiously asked him if the tea was "piss-poor." Not understanding the term, the wallah answered, "Yes, sahib," and so the tea became "piss-poor" tea, which name he proudly proclaimed as he walked the aisles. He also sold "Charlie Chaplin" tea for similar reasons.

We found a Chinese restaurant outside the gates

where we could eat very reasonably. Whenever Lee accompanied us, they gave us a fifty-percent discount and served us in the officers' section. Another cheap place to eat was an Indian restaurant where water buffalo steaks and tomatoes, or hamburgers and tomatoes were served for a rupee (30 cents). However, we stopped patronizing that place for two reasons. One was that we ran out of money, and two was that some GI reported seeing the Indian cooks forming the hamburger patties by pressing them under their armpits.

One day we heard bagpipes being played and rushed to the parade grounds in time to see the native troops in review. They marched to the skirl of the bagpipes played by a Sikh detachment bedecked in tartan. To an American GI it looked like something out of "Gunga Din" or "Beau Geste" as they paraded around the grounds passing in front of the British officers reviewing the troops.

After about a week we were loaded into third-class,

unlit, wooden railroad cars of the Bengal-Nagpur Railroad. Benches ran the length of the cars with luggage racks above them. In the vestibule at the end of the car the floor was pierced with a hole. Two bricks were strategically placed adjacent to it. We would have to use this device several times during our journey. My initiation came on the first evening around midnight. With only the moonlight to guide me, I inadvertently mounted the bricks in the wrong direction, and although I always aim to please, I entirely missed the hole.

For three-and-a-half days we railroaded across India, passing through jungles with monkeys cavorting in the trees, open countryside, and through railroad yards of bustling cities, the largest of which was Nagpur, halfway across the country.

As we pulled into the yard, the train halted near a water tank, used to replenish locomotives. One enterprising GI decided a shower was in order. He disrobed, crossed the tracks to the tank and wet himself down by pulling on the chain that controlled the flow of water. He let up on the chain and proceeded to lather himself from head to toe. Alas! Before he could rinse off, the train started to pull out. With foam spewing from his body, he legged it down the tracks in hot pursuit while we leaned out the windows shouting encouragement until in a last desperate lunge, he pulled himself aboard the last car. One can't help but wonder what he would have done if he were stranded in the middle of India wearing nothing but his dog tags!

Food was either bad or nonexistent. Occasionally the train would stop for everyone to fall out and do calisthenics. Then the "cooks" would walk the track delivering the food-de-jour. Cases of food would be thrown out of each coach, along with bread sometimes. One meal consisted of cans of maple syrup, several loaves of bread and two-gallon cans of sauerkraut! Bon Appetit. We tasted one can of sauerkraut and donated the foul stuff to a blind beggar seated near the tracks. He gingerly tasted it and instantly spat it out, convincing us that here was one food that should have never been invented.

Sleeping was difficult. Not only were the wooden benches hard and uncomfortable, but there wasn't enough room for everyone to stretch out, not only on the benches but also on the floor. Some guys even slept in the luggage racks. We were not sorry to off-load our weary bodies when at last the train made a final stop in a field below our next base. Boys offered to carry our duffles up the slope to the camp. For half a rupee they struggled up the hill with a bag on their heads. One enterprising lad tried for a whole rupee by carrying two bags, but as we placed the second on his head, he sank into the ground.

As one Bill Shakespeare might say, "Double duffle, toil and trouble." (No, I guess he wouldn't!).

We were billeted in Indian-style thatch-roofed

barracks of bamboo and plaster at Charra, an airfield near the town of Purulia, some 150 miles west of Calcutta. Purulia was in the midst of a smallpox epidemic, which didn't prevent us from skinny dipping with the water buffaloes in a stream below the village, under the eyes of the village matrons seated along the banks. At first I was reluctant to join in, but then I shed my scruples along with my clothes and enjoyed a cooling dip -- just one more bare ass in the crowd.

India proved to be dusty and hot. The March-April weather equivalent to our hot summers. What would real summer be like? Fortunately, I was not to find out, for requests were made for volunteers to proceed to an advance base in China. I broke down and broke my "no volunteer" rule for a second time, thus making what proved to be the wisest decision of my army career. I jumped at the opportunity to see China!

CHAPTER 5
OVER THE HUMP

I said good-bye to Lee and Fitzgerald, Murphy and the rest of the guys and found myself with a group of twenty seated in a C-46 cargo plane in two rows of bucket seats. Strapped to the floor between the seats were twenty 55-gallon drums of aviation fuel. Everyone and everything were bound for the same "secret" destination. We flew northward up the Assam River Valley, in what is now East Pakistan, to the remote village of Sadiya near the Burmese border and the Japs. After refueling, we took off again and climbed 21,000 feet to fly over the Hump, the GI's name for the Himalaya Mountains. At this altitude we passed mountain peaks that soared higher than we, through the white blanket of clouds below. In spite of fleece-lined clothes, we were uncomfortably cold in the unheated plane. The temperature outside registered at twenty degrees below zero. Breathing became difficult when the oxygen ran out.

We landed in Kunming, in southern China, to spend

the night. Next morning, we flew north, landing at A-1, one of the four large forward bases in the vicinity of Chengdu. From there we flew north a short distance to A-3, which would be our new station, four miles east of the walled city of Kwanghan. A small group of locals greeted our arrival, obviously curious about Americans, so seldom seen in this remote area of the world. We were equally curious.

They wore gray and blue coats and straw sandals. Some had on turban-like hats and smoked long bamboo pipes. They offered us gifts of sugar cane as a gesture of greeting. We were trucked to hostel #2, a half mile along a dirt road past lush green rice paddies, inquisitive people gawking as we passed. We were billeted in pyramidal tents with cement floors,, each tent containing four cots and a small coal stove. A nucleus of bamboo and plaster tile-roofed buildings in the center of the area provided facilities for a headquarters, mess hall, laundry, bath house, day room, hostel office, company store and a generator that would eventually free us from illumination by candlelight.

It came as a big surprise to learn that my duties were to drive a large truck called a 6 by 6 for a group that was classified as an "alert crew." Somehow my M.O. had me down for that capacity, although the only thing I had driven up to that time was a little hangar-tug back in Great Bend where I taught myself the mysteries of motoring. When I confessed to my lack of ability, they made a substitution and my new duties were related to refueling, namely rolling and decanting gasoline drums into our storage facilities and conversely using these facilities to refuel transient aircraft. It turned out to be a herculean task for each drum weighed 350 lbs. and the distances they were to be rolled could be as much as a quarter of a mile. The resistance of the sloshing liquid inside prevented them from rolling smoothly. At their destination, they had to be uplifted, opened, and then poured into a trough to be pumped into one of the four giant gas tanks stationed about the field. Struggling with oil drums was even more difficult as each weighed 450 lbs. and had to be hand lifted into weapons-carriers to be transported to the oil revetment. Needless to say, muscles were rapidly developed doing this sort of work. Even so, Charles Atlas I was not.

Besides bombs, our B-29s ferried gas over the hump in bomb-bay tanks which had to be drained into open drums placed below the tanks. From here, the gas was pumped along the pipeline to the storage tanks. The fumes from the cascading gas could give you a good high. This operation gave us the opportunity to do our laundry, as nothing cleans oily clothes better than 100 octane gasoline. We would just toss our fatigues into the drum of swirling gas. Another trick was to hang our canteens in the cold gasoline. It was a great way to put a chill into our drinking water, whose cloudy origin from a Chinese well had been tempered by boiling and then cooling, then doctored with iodine and placed in a pungent Lister bag. Cooling made it infinitely more palatable. The Chinese called the brew "Lin Kai Sway," Cold Boiled Water.

I took every opportunity offered me to drive the jeep and weapons-carrier (4 x 4), and fool around with the 6 x 6, and so I was able to show the motor pool Captain my new found (self-taught) abilities, for which he rewarded me with a license.

The reason we were in China was to maintain forward bases from which the B-29s could reach and bomb the lower islands of Japan. Before a mission could be pulled from the four forward bases in China, gas, oil and bombs had to be ferried up in sufficient quantity to get the B-29s to Japan and back, and then get them back to the home bases in India. It would take a concerted two-or-three-weeks effort for B-29s and cargo planes to amass these needed supplies. During this time, the planes were operating from our four rear bases in India, bombing the

Japs in Burma, Thailand, Malaysia, and Singapore.

The B-29 was capable of carrying forty 500 lb. bombs, but due to the distances involved in our theatre of operations, twenty bombs were the maximum carried. These were slung on racks in two bomb bays and were dropped electronically in a sequence that could be set into the mechanism, so that they could be dropped selectively or jettisoned in one large cluster. In practice the bombs would all be dropped in unison with the lead bomber so that the one bombardier would zero in on the target. Once the bombardier set the Norden bombsight for the target, the plane would be flown on automatic pilot, guided only by the bombsight mechanism, and no deviation from course could occur until after the bombs were dropped.

If in an emergency the bombs had to be jettisoned in friendly territory, they could be dropped safely by having the arming wire latch open up, thus dropping the bomb with the wire in place. This would prevent the arming of the fuse. However, composition "B" bombs started to be used, which were said to detonate without a fuse, so in theory, the bombs could not be dropped safely. At any rate, they began wiring the arming wire in such a way that it was impossible to drop the bomb without pulling the safety wire and arming the fuse. Perhaps it was to avoid any malfunctioning of the system. They wanted to be absolutely sure that the bombs would explode on contact. When the bombs were ferried up to us for storage, they would be dropped two at a time from the bomb bay -- often from ten feet -- and would hit the ground with a resounding thud. None ever went off. One incident in India gave us something to think about. Several GIs were killed, and a plane destroyed while they were loading anti-personnel cluster bombs for a mission to Burma.

The B-29 carried a total of fourteen calibre-50 machine guns and a 20mm cannon in five-gun turrets. They were controlled remotely by electronic gun sight from four-gun stations (top, two sides and tail), and by the bombardier in the nose. The controls could be passed to one another as needed. The plane's speed of 350 mph was fast enough to allow a Jap Zero to make only one pass. This gave the tail gunner a great opportunity to shoot it down with his cannon.

One of our planes actually got on the tail of a slower model Jap plane and shot it down over Burma. The bewildered Jap pilot bailed out. One of the first B-29s to fly over the hump encountered an inquisitive British fighter plane over Burma. When the unidentified plane flew in close for a look-see, our boys shot the "bandit" down, the pilot hitting the silk. As if that wasn't bad enough, the B-29 crew wanted to credit themselves with the kill by adding a British flag on the side of the ship reserved for Jap flags which proclaimed their martial accomplishments. Incidentally, each hump flight entitled them to a painted camel, and each mission, a painted bomb.

The summer ushered in mosquito time. Those pesky little anopheles mosquitoes came out every evening bent on inoculating everyone with malaria. Repellant applied to exposed parts of the body discouraged attack. At night we slept under mosquito netting and fell asleep to the tune of whining mosquitoes trying to get in bed with us. One half of our base eventually came down with malaria. Of course, all the Chinese had it, but it seemed to affect them similarly to a bad cold. The GIs, however, were hospital cases, not having built up any resistance or immunity to the disease.

By June 15th enough supplies were on hand to pull the first B-29 raid on Japan from our advanced bases in China -- the first bombing of mainland Japan since the Doolittle raid from Navy aircraft carriers in 1942. Our planes arrived on the 14th, after which the entire night was spent refueling the planes. Particularly difficult was the topping off of the oil tanks. Each of the four engines on a plane was equipped with a tank of 80 gallons of oil, half of which had been consumed on the plane's flight from India. This meant that about two-thirds of a drum of oil had to be added to each engine on a dozen planes. The only method to do this was bucket by bucket, passed from the ground up to the wing where it could be poured through a funnel into the tank. Tex Johnston, my tent mate, and I ferried oil drums from the revetment on a weapons carrier and then proceeded to slop around in the dark with our messy, back-breaking task, sometimes getting more oil on ourselves than in the tank. By dawn we were finished and then started helping to top off the gas tanks using the gasoline supplied through the pipeline from the storage tanks.

This was really just a monitoring job, and I promptly fell asleep lying on the wing, while the tank was filling. Our chief woke me and sent me back to my tent, and as I fell asleep I could hear the roar as the planes started to take off on their epic flight. That evening, after they all arrived safely back at the field, we had to go back through the same ridiculous procedure so that they could fly back to India the next morning. In the three-week hiatus before the second mission, some inventive GI converted the winch assembly on a 6 x 6 into an oil pump, so that the oil could be pumped directly from the drums sitting on the truck through a hose into the tanks up on the wings. They should have given that guy a medal!

Bomb runs were usually carried out at altitudes of 20,000 feet. Cloudy conditions usually prevailed, which necessitated bombing by radar. Misses by several miles from the target were not uncommon. General Curtis "Iron Pants" LeMay ordered low-level bombing, which provided better results but more crew casualties. The B-29s could only reach the most southern island of Japan from our bases in China. Therefore, the bombing of Tokyo had to remain on the waiting list.

After each raid, a stripped-down photo-recon plane (with no guns or turrets), its bomb bays loaded with extra gas in bomb-bay tanks, would be sent to photograph both the results of the bombing mission and new potential targets. By taking off at midnight, they would be over Japan early in the morning. This would give them sufficient time to complete their mission and be back at base before dark. They could fly very high, and their stripped-down streamlining would enable them to outrun any pursuing Zero, while their lone armament, the cannon in the tail, would help to discourage any Jap pilot who managed to get close.

One night we were readying planes that had returned from a mission for their trip back to India the next morning. A plane roared towards us through the darkness, its head lights lighting up the runway. It lifted slowly as it passed by us and disappeared into the night. We returned to our chores when suddenly the whole sky lit up with an orange hue. The recon plane had crashed in a ball of fire, its 9,000 gallons of gasoline fueling an inferno that burned for hours. When the flames subsided, all that was left were four battered engines, the landing gear strut, and the broken-off tail assembly. The rest of the metal plane had been completely consumed in the intense conflagration. One GI miraculously escaped death.

Fortunately, the plane had cleared the village, four miles off the end of the runway, and crashed in a rice paddy. The plane probably either lost power or the pilot tried to gain altitude too soon, a no-no in a heavily laden B-29. I saw one of our planes do the same thing while taking off in India. It pulled up too quickly and nearly mushed right into the ground, only just missing a fatal crash by the proverbial inch.

Our field, and the three others in the area like it, were constructed entirely by hand, using 100,000 coolies at each site. No concrete was used, but rather a slurry of clay poured over up-ended river stones in three layers, large ones on the bottom, smaller ones in the middle, and small ones on top. Over this, tung oil was spread, after the heavy rollers had been pulled by human "horses" back and forth over the surface to pack it solid. Each field consisted of a mile and-a-half runway, one hundred feet wide, with two encircling taxi strips sixty feet wide, each strip with innumerable circular parking bays for not only our B-29s but also for transient cargo planes and a squadron of P-47 fighter planes, which was also based at our field. All these strips were capable of supporting the tremendous weight of a fully loaded B-29, some 140,000 pounds. When a plane ran off the pavement and mired in the soft clay, its wheels sinking several feet into the muck, who else but the alert crew had to dig it out and winch it back onto hard ground.

Recruited Chinese laborers were still working on the field, patching, and finishing here and there, sometimes endangering themselves in the process. They had a penchant for running across the path of any moving vehicle, narrowly averting a collision. In so doing they believed they were killing the evil dragon that followed them. An error in judgment occasionally cost them their lives as was evident one day when I heard a landing fighter pilot in communication with the tower say over the loudspeaker, "I just got another coolie."

Our field was situated in a beautiful valley in Szechuan Province in the interior of China. The flat valley stretched from a ridge to the east westward toward a distant mountain range, its lofty 25,000-foot summit visible to us only once during our stay. The lush valley, with the able assistance of human fertilizer, supported two crops a year of rice, cotton and soybeans in irrigated paddy fields which were divided by walls that also provided pathways through the flooded fields. The country smelled like a gigantic latrine at manure-spreading time when a slurry of the "honey" that had cured in water all winter long was ladled and flung about the landscape.

Gasoline for our motor vehicles became scarce and

it became necessary for our Commander, Colonel Clarke to curtail unnecessary use of transportation. All personnel, including the Commander himself, were obliged to walk to and from the field. A short cut led us along rice paddy walls that wound between fields of rice and over irrigation ditches.

One day an unearthly cry of terror filled the air, prompting me to investigate the source. The sound emanated from the midst of a group of farmers watching the slaughtering of a pig, whose primordial cries slowly subsided as the tethered beast slowly bled to death. He was on his back, blood pouring from a gash in his throat to a catch basin below. The local butcher was presiding over the ceremony. He proceeded to cut a hole above the ankle bone of a rear leg, and then pass a steel rod through the opening and up the leg between the skin and the flesh, separating one from the other as he worked the rod up and around the animal's torso, eventually loosening the skin around the entire pig.

Removing the rod, he then put his mouth to the hole and proceeded to inflate the pig, balloon fashion, by blowing air into the chamber created by the rod manipulation. Slowly the scrawny animal rounded out into a taut puffball even as the "yellow" butcher's face brightened to a vivid scarlet. He then plugged the hole with a wooden peg to prevent leakage. That done, the farmers rolled and scraped the carcass free of hair. The next day the animal would hang in small strips from meat hooks outside the butcher's open stall along the dusty road to Kwanghan.

There was only one road which led from a little town one mile to our east named San Sze Gwan, past our hostel Westward four more miles to the walled town of Kwanghan, then north or south. To the south five miles away was the walled town of Sin Tu and another five miles further the large city of Chengdu, known as the university city, because of its many colleges.

A stream wandered along the northern perimeter of our airfield. It was a small arm of an irrigation project that had been created a thousand years before by diverting the flow of a mountain river into the whole valley. From this new waterway the valley was irrigated through a system of streams and canals so that water was abundant in any season. One day we ran our jeep out into the stream to give it a good wash when along came a sampan being pulled downstream. Our vehicle blocked its transit. The jeep wouldn't start with its exhaust under water, and the gondolier had to wait until we could push the jeep out of his way. It was probably the first traffic tie-up of its kind in history – "gridlock" Chinese- American style.

While decanting gasoline drums one day with the help of a squad of Chinese soldiers who were also assigned to the task, their squad leader came over and with sign language challenged me to a foot race. What the hell, I accepted the challenge. We laid out a course of about one hundred yards and at a signal we raced down the course pretty much neck and neck until the last few yards. At the finish line I won by a Roman nose. After catching his breath, the loser challenged me to a rematch. This time he removed his straw sandals and ran barefoot. We raced over the course and I managed to nose him out once more. After resting, he challenged me a third time, but it had to be a barefoot race. Laughingly, I refused. There was no way I could run shoeless over that pebbly surface. The Chinese saved face by my refusal, and everyone had a good laugh over the whole event.

My speed afoot helped on another occasion when a GI working with me on the line casually mentioned, "Look at that crazy C-46 taxiing to take off with its rudder locked." I could see the red wooden block that had been tightened on the rudder to prevent it from moving while the plane was parked. If the plane took off handicapped in this way, steering would be possible only by banking the plane slowly using the ailerons, and it would be almost impossible to keep it lined up on the runway during landing, especially in a cross wind. Although the pilot should test his controls before taking off, he just might not. Deciding that he should be warned, I found myself in a foot race with the plane. Taking a diagonal course across the field to intercept him at the head of the runway, a quarter of a mile away, I made it to the plane before he started to take off. He saw me waving my arms but couldn't hear my shouts over the roar of the engines. He got his crew chief to open the back door to see what the hell the shouting was about. The chief quickly removed the lock, a job that was his responsibility in the first place.

One night the Japs came over to pay us a visit. I was out on the taxi strip when the alert sounded. The fighter planes took off to see if they could intercept anything in the dark sky overhead. We could hear them circling around, at least we thought they were our friendly aircraft when suddenly the bombs started to fall. A string of them burst in the distance on the taxi strip on which we were standing. Each explosion came closer, heading right down the strip toward us. Panic struck. I ran in a small circle and dropped in the mud awaiting the worst, but the enemy ran out of bombs before he reached us and harmlessly flew over our heads. Well, I was up and away from that field in short order. As a GI would say, "I got my ass out of there" and headed down a road and into a ditch, where I remained until such time as I could resume the dignity I had so recently lost.

The guy sharing my ditch was no help. He actually shook the whole time, and later, when air raids became routine, he'd disappear at the first alert, while the enemy was a hundred miles away. The rest of us at least waited for the two ball fifty-mile alert before seeking haven among burial mounds in a Chinese cemetery. From that vantage point among the ancestors, we could watch the fireworks in comparative safety. Once we heard the rumble of bombs going off twenty miles south of us at A-1, which seemed to get hit more often than we. Suddenly a ball of flame burst in the sky in that direction. A P-61 Black Widow night fighter had shot down a Jap bomber over A-1.

One night the Japs knocked out three P-51s on our field, together with some gas drums, machine-gunning our tent area to boot. On another night, a newly assigned top sergeant showed more than the normal amount of concern, as we lay in the cemetery waiting for something to happen, while kidding around to kill time. When we heard a plane overhead, probably one of ours, he told us to lie still and not to make any noise lest the enemy see or hear us in the dark. I wondered how this was possible and concluded that this old-time regular army man was a little chicken. He soon transferred back to India. Later the poor guy walked into a spinning prop and was chopped to pieces.

One day Colonel Clarke came up behind me as I was reading the bulletin board to absorb some inconsequential information, such as the rationing of toilet paper to six sheets a day. He said, "Soldier, don't you have another pair of pants to wear?" I knew what he was alluding to, for indeed one of my bare cheeks protruded from a jagged hole in the seat of my oil-splattered fatigues, since I had long since given up the practice of wearing underwear. Since no replacement fatigues were obtainable from our meagerly supplied quartermaster, I was forced to donate one of my Class A britches to the war effort in "operation cover up."

Driving was hazardous, as pedestrians were continually zig-zagging from one side of the road to the other in front of the vehicles in an attempt to kill their dragons. One unlucky farmer, out on the road at night during an air raid alert, was struck by a blacked-out truck and was found lying dead in the road in front of our hostel the next morning.

It was difficult to impress upon the Chinese the respect they should reserve for moving vehicles. This was apparent one day when on a stormy afternoon our planes started to arrive back from a mission. With the weather causing problems, they suddenly emerged out of the clouds on their approach to the runway. At the time, a long line of coolies was doing the "coolie shuffle" across the runway, dirt slung in baskets on poles across their shoulders. Someone in the tower said, "Clear those coolies off the runway." I took it upon myself to run down to where they were and to hold up the line every time a plane dropped out of the clouds.

Suddenly, as one plane made its approach, two dogs ran onto the runway and were run over by the plane. As another plane started its approach, some coolies from the other side of the runway ran out, and, in spite of my shouts, grabbed the kicking dogs and started to drag them off. They had risked their lives for a dinner of roasted dog. Yes, it's true -- the Chinese eat anything that moves and most things that don't. The Chinese soldiers shot and killed our orderly room mascot, little "Boo Doong" (Don't Understand) and carried him, suspended from a pole, off to their cook pot. On another occasion, I declined a Chinese's invitation to shoot his dog.

The disregard of danger cost another coolie his life when after an air raid he picked up a small unexploded anti-personnel bomb and tossed it to his friend. After that same raid, while driving back to the base with Glad (who had won the truck driver assignment that I had to relinquish) he showed me his trophy. Pouncing around in the glove compartment of his 6 x 6 was a foot-long bomb with the arming propeller precariously unwound halfway. We were in more danger from ourselves than from the Japs!

This became apparent one day when I was checking

the oil revetment. I heard the crack of a rifle and a buzz go past my ear. Ducking down behind an oil drum, I cautiously peered out toward the source of the sound. Here came Plunkett over the revetment wall carrying his carbine, out for a day of shooting. This was the same good old Plunkett who, back in the States, had washed out of bombardier school when he inadvertently dropped a practice bomb on a gas station outside the bombing range.

A funny thing happened to me one day while I was alone under a plane's bomb bay, siphoning gas into an open drum. The tank coupling was overhead and as I opened it 100 octane gas ran down my arm and my bare chest into my pants and scored a direct hit on the family jewels. Turpentine on a dog's butt couldn't have hurt more. I let out a yell, dropped my pants and started fanning the vital parts, all of my clothes around my ankles. Who picked that moment to drive up in a jeep -- the base Commander! He glanced at me, but before I could offer an explanation, he chucked a pipe wrench at my feet, said "give this to the master sergeant," and drove off leaving me standing there balls-ass naked, turning an embarrassing shade of red.

The day came when Major Warden, our new CO, called me into his office and asked me why I hated the army. He was surprised when I replied that he was mistaken, and that I was as content as anyone could be under the circumstances. He had checked my service record and upon finding my IQ score was 150, he figured someone at that level really must be fed up rolling oil drums. And so, he assigned me to Lieutenant Cohen, statistical officer on the field. From now on I would no longer roll drums, I would count them. A jeep was provided and once a day my job was to count all full gasoline drums on the field, stick-gage four storage tanks, count replacement engines, make a count of Chinese soldiers working on the field, and bring all figures to the Lieutenant for his daily report.

A secondary job arose. Lt. Cohen wanted to learn how to drive his jeep and it fell upon me to try to teach him, a simple task normally, but not the case with this student. His total lack of coordination nearly crashed us into the operations shack wall. Another of Lt. Cohen's ambitions was to become a Captain, because his father would be proud of such an achievement. When told by the Major that our group's authorization for that rank was complete, the Lieutenant had the audacity to suggest a transfer to an outfit that had that rank open, so that after he obtained his Captaincy, he could be transferred back. His scheme was not acceptable to the Major.

One day a letter arrived with the sad news that my brother George, who was four years my senior and had been in the army since January 1940, had been killed on July 19, 1944 in mopping up operations after the taking of Saipan, an island in the Pacific. Sad as this news was, my sorrow was increased that much more when I learned that my father had suffered a heart condition as a result and had passed away on August 24th, two weeks after hearing about the tragic loss of his son. Subsequently my mother informed me that, since I was the last male in the family, she had contacted the Red Cross to have me transferred back to the States. This would get me a short visit with my family, which would be great, but after that, what? Stateside army life with all its chicken shit was not for me. The relaxed atmosphere of overseas duty, together with the adventure of foreign lands, far outweighed being stationed in Oshkosh, B'Gosh, trying to be a good Boy Scout. I implored my mother to let me stay in China, impressing upon her the comparative safety of my assignment there. She acquiesced, much to my relief.

On August 20th, the B-29s were arriving back from a daylight raid as dusk was setting in. Colonel Warden had just landed and deplaned, and I was talking to him, as another B-29 approached the runway at too high an elevation to make a landing. The Colonel said, "that's Major Hansen's plane," as it turned for the long circle around for a second try. As we continued to talk, there was an orange flash in the sky over the hills to our east. Major Hansen had crashed into them on the final turn for his approach to the runway. There was very little flame since there was precious little fuel left to burn. It was later ascertained that as he banked in his turn, the little gas remaining in his wing tanks drained away from the pumps in his lowered wing and his left engines cut out, dipping him into the hill. The crash scattered his plane for a thousand feet along the top of the ridge, the tail traveling the farthest and ending up facing the wrong way. One man survived.

Next morning a weapons carrier was rolling out of the yard and hearing that they were on their way to the wreck, I jumped aboard. I joined a group of officers and enlisted men and a Chinese gentleman who would act as an interpreter. We took the narrow service road that ran eastward from the field and drove between rice paddy fields and across planks spanning irrigation ditches. We passed huge bamboo water wheels which were slowly turned by a stream below to lift water to a sluice above.

The road took us to a point three miles east of the runway, where a radar tent was manned to guide the B-29s back from their missions. The road ended at a river. We left the weapons carrier and crossed the river on a flat-bottomed ferry. We waded ashore and headed along narrow paths through the lush countryside for four miles, until we sighted the wreck. I was glad to relieve myself of my burden -- a five-gallon can of water that I had lugged the four miles from the river. Someone else had toted a case of "C" rations.

The wreck sight was encircled by gawking Chinese and their families. None of the wreck had burned, but it had broken up completely into large jagged sections of metal and lay scattered along the hilltop along with the bodies of the crew.

Suddenly the purpose of our mission became apparent. The bodies had yet to be brought out, and we were here to collect them. Only the lone injured GI had been taken out the night before. The smell of death was in the air. Someone recognized Major Hansen's body, although the head was missing. The Captain found his scalp forty feet away. One of his legs was cut off at the thigh and the broken bone protruded beyond the cut, reminding me of an Easter ham. His body was not rigid, as the other bodies proved to be. Every bone in his body must have been broken. We wrapped him in a parachute cloth. One body protruded from beneath a large piece of sheet metal and as I raised the metal up I could see that his head was gone. His chest was split open and his heart protruded. Another had the top of his head sliced off clean as a whistle, his hollow half-skull devoid of brains. One man's leg was crushed so that a portion was mere strings from which his foot dangled. Four severed legs were picked up and assigned to each corpse that lacked one, no effort being made to pair them properly.

Ten corpses wrapped in white nylon parachutes now awaited transport. There was no way our small party could accomplish this. It was all we could do to lift their dead weight and gather them together. Now it was the Chinese interpreter's turn to act. He organized teams of porters and conscripted reluctant farmers to do the job. The bodies were slung from bamboo poles like hunter's prey and the somber safari began.

On the way back we rested on a paddy wall and the accompanying coolies with their macabre burden paused to rest with us. I had been carrying the unopened case of "C" rations and the pause gave me the opportunity to break into it and open a can of franks and beans and a can of crackers with my trench knife, thereby enjoying some nourishment, even though the fare resembled blood and guts.

Our coolies were regular porters and carried a contraption consisting of two bamboo poles with a seat hanging between. They had folded the seat down flat and laid the body on top of the rig, which they carried over both shoulders rather comfortably. They signaled for me to put the case of rations alongside the body and trotted off ahead of me as we continued on our way.

Farther down the road, I ran into the Captain and the interpreter who were resting on a paddy wall. I cut a piece of sugar cane from an adjacent field and sat down with them. As we quenched our thirst, a farmer with rake in hand appeared and protested. The interpreter yanked out a very-pistol that he had taken from the wreck and pointed the large-bore flare gun at the farmer whose slant eyes actually became round! Throwing his rake straight into the air, he high- tailed it away and around the end of the row of cane, disappearing from sight. A few minutes later his head and one arm reappeared, and he gestured for us to help ourselves.

Finally, we reached the ferry, and after crossing the river, the coolies laid the bodies down on the ground and lined up for their pay. The interpreter, now acting as pay master, gave each pair of porters the prearranged amount. This didn't please the porters who had accompanied me. They had gone the whole distance, while many of the others were more recent replacements for porters who had dropped out along the way. But like the parable in the gospel about the laborers in the vineyard, each man received the same amount regardless of his degree of labor.

We loaded our gruesome cargo onto the bed of our truck, like cord wood, stacked one above the other, with me inside the covered truck guiding the stiff and stubborn bodies into a neat pile. We all rode back on the front end, sitting on the fenders and hood, away from the unpleasant odor in the rear. Next morning, in a shelter out on the line, we came across a stack of pine boxes awaiting final transportation to the cemetery in Chengdu, maggots already falling out of the cracks in the boxes.

One of the movies that played the base was "Arsenic and Old Lace," which depicted two old ladies and their crazy brother who thought he was Teddy Roosevelt at San Juan Hill. He would yell "Charge!" at the top of his voice as he raced up the stairs. At the time the movie hit the base, I was sporting a walrus moustache. In fact, Major Warden had taken a keen interest in its growth and had delighted in showing me off to visiting personnel on more than one occasion. During the run of the movie, at the moment Teddy charged up the stairs, our master sergeant jumped up and shouted "Fisher" and from that moment on they called me "Teddy" or "Mr. President." For a long time thereafter, I was expected to yell "Charge!" every time someone greeted me with my new name.

When we arrived in China, the black-market rate of

exchange was two hundred to one, and Yuan could be bought very easily. However, the American government was paying the Chinese government for our keep, including rent, food, and care at the official rate of forty to one...five times the realistic rate. By the time we left China later, the street rate had risen to five hundred to one...twelve times the official rate.

The Chinese people were hoarding American dollars and Indian rupees as a hedge against inflation. One enterprising GI became a money dealer in his spare time. He set up a table in the compound and exchanged money with the transient gun crews at a nice profit to himself. Captain Peast opened up a store, and sold souvenirs supplied to him by some enterprising entrepreneurs of Kwanghan. The profits were supposedly intended for squadron equipment and activities, benefits that didn't materialize. He was transferred and months later we got word of the arrest of Captain Peast for profiteering.

There were other criminal activities at the base. A gunner noticed a small pilot chute, which is used to deploy the main chute when the rip cord is yanked, lying in a ditch alongside his plane. Investigation of the parachutes in the plane revealed one pack minus a chute, an army blanket in its place, good only for a long sleep for any unsuspecting user. Chute nylon was in demand, for it provided local women with material for making and embroidering beautiful ladies' blouses. The culprit was never caught.

One GI flashed a pile of silver rupees at me one day. He was apprehended when gunners complained about coins missing from their money belts. These belts were issued for the sole purpose of survival, and contained 30 silver rupees sewn into individual pockets, along with pointie-talkie books in local languages. The belts were critical to survival in case of bailout, the money often used to buy one's way to freedom. One of our boys landed in the middle of a river, and the would-be rescuers circled him in canoes crying "Rupee, rupee," waiting for assurance that they would be paid.

A more amusing incident happened one night. I had pulled duty as Charge of Quarters and after midnight, as there was nothing to do until morning except answer the field phone if it rang, I crawled into a cot with the phone pack for a pillow, and promptly fell asleep. But not for long. Glad came in and woke me up to tell me that his wallet had been stolen and thrown in a ten-holer, minus the money. He wanted me to wake up Major Warden to have the wallet checked for fingerprints! When I told him, he was out of his mind and if he wanted to speak to the Major he had better in hell wake him up himself, he stormed out with that intention. I never heard anything more about it.

Confrontations of a violent nature are often the result of differences of opinion that are expressed with too much vehemence. You must learn to temper your language if you don't want to back your argument with your fists.

Not being a belligerent person, I found myself in the unenviable position of eating crow when challenged to settle an argument with my dukes. I had been appreciatively irate with Newman, and my harangue raised that pug's hackles. I was mad enough to fight him but knew that it just wouldn't be the Christian thing to do. So, I didn't stand up to meet him. He stormed off into the night, the apparent winner in a match of brawn over brain. It's a miserable feeling to bear, realizing that your fellow GIs probably put you down for being chicken.

Some days later, I pulled Charge of Quarters. One of my duties was to waken certain personnel in the early hours of the morning. Newman was on my list, and I wondered if I would have to face another challenge. Sure enough, he gave me a hard time and refused to roll out of the sack. Instead of making a scene, I simply said to him that if he refused, I would put him on report for disobeying a direct order. After all, I outranked him by one stripe, and was CQ to boot. He got out of bed, a victim of brain over brawn.

About this time, I received a letter from home telling me of the passing of Mr. Chips, our family's cocker spaniel. Shortly thereafter, a "Dear John" letter arrived from Muriel announcing her marriage to another GI on leave. The cumulative effect of losing my brother, my father, my dog, and my girl in that order must have taken a little of the euphoria out of living, but not for long. Life is too precious to dwell on misfortune.

There was another ugly thing going on, sabotage, not by GIs, but by local Chinese or Jap spies. During one air raid, fires were lit off the east end of the runway as a guide for the Jap bombers and we could hear our planes strafing the spot. At the other end of the runway, four miles away from town, a homing beacon was discovered that the Japs could tune into to find the field. On another occasion, a saboteur opened the drain valve on one of our large tanks of gasoline and a thousand gallons of that precious $35-a-gallon fluid drained into an irrigation ditch before someone discovered it and shut the valve.

We waded around in the dark for hours, skimming the surface of the water with portable pumps, all the while hoping that the spark arrestors on the exhaust pipes wouldn't ignite the strong fumes. Water was pumped into the tank along with the gas. Later, after the water had settled to the bottom of the tank, it was drained off.

On our days off, we usually went to Kwanghan, walking the four miles or riding in a rickshaw behind a sweaty dog-trotting muscular specimen of the human race, the rickshaw coolie. They say that they are short-lived, and it pains me to think that perhaps my heavy weight hastened their demise. They walked along up the few rises in the road, trotting the rest of the distance without a break. The four hundred Chinese dollars ($2.00 American) they asked for this service seems little enough but bear in mind that I only drew about $29 a month and seldom could afford this luxury. I never rode back to the base, for the wily Chinese, once they got you to town, would not bring you home for less than eight hundred Chinese dollars.

Along the way we passed shy ladies shielding their faces with fans from American eyes; men shuffling along with baskets of tangerines slung on carrying poles; a wheelbarrow containing a squealing pig, tied with its feet in the air, being trundled to market by a struggling farmer with a strap across his shoulders that support the barrow's handles; another barrow returning from town, its pig replaced by a seated lady shielding her face with a fan as she's taxied along the road; a small family cemetery with its cluster of mounds, eroded on one side with rotted coffins and bones exposed; small stands with fruits and nuts, sandals and wine for sale; a traveler, his bare buttocks exposed as he squats and relieves himself alongside the road; a sick man, crouching, his swollen leg dripping fluid;

a pharmaceutical stand where salved patches can be pasted

on any pained part

Sometimes they'll push a pig to market that way, the big fat porker on his back, tied to a bed of straw. It's also amusing to see a herd of ducks coming down the road with a shepherd armed with a bamboo switch to drive them.

But the most amusing of all is to see a little chinese boy taking a huge water buffalo out for an airing along the rice paddy walks. I've never seen a little water buffalo!

of the body; a sedan chair with its occupant completely

concealed within, being transported by four bearers to her

wedding, amidst a din of bells clanging to announce the

occasion to all travelers on the road..

The main gate to the town is set in the twenty-foot- high wall below a drum tower which commands the entrance. The road threads its way through the archway in the thick wall past the open massive door, swung back on its rusted hinges. Passing walled courtyards, the road leads into the commercial center of the town. Bisecting streets humming with activity, each street devoted to a separate industry. Candle makers dip their tapers into vats of steaming wax; noodle makers dry their product on poles overhanging the street; furniture makers fashion their bamboo into chairs and tables; the tinsmiths produce teapots and utensils out of discarded GI food cans; cutlery makers display an unusual assortment of knives and scissors; embroiderers decorate silks with exotic dragons and even the coffin makers have their own street to practice their somber trade.

At convenient locations along the main route, clusters of natives huddle in dim interiors, rice bowls held under their chins, partaking of their daily sustenance.

These food shops waft their tantalizing odors into

the narrow passages, there to blend with all the other strange smells -- melted wax, tanned leathers, open latrines, tethered pigs, etc. The combined odors prompt a hasty advance through the town to the gate ahead, where, outside the wall, one can cleanse one's lungs and clear one's head before attempting the long dash back through the town.

This system of segregating trades made comparison shopping easy, but each merchant set his price and would not bargain -- at least not with a GI. However, a Chinese could get it for you at a lower price. Wherever we went, we GIs were followed, like the Pied Piper by Chinese children who would crowd around the shop windows looking in at us as we tried to strike a bargain, shouting at us and the shopkeeper in their strange gibberish. Little tots played in the streets; their diaper problem solved by the ingenious Chinese who simply slit the open their pants so all they had to do was squat!

Once more back through the town and out the main

gate, we could opt for walking four miles back to the base or paying the $800 escalated price to be rickshawed. At those prices, I opted to walk.

One day, halfway home, I had a strong desire to be alone, away from the multitude, if only to sit quietly and eat my bagful of plums. I cut through a graveyard alongside the road, and nestled down between its burial mounds, which provided sanctuary from the bustle of the road. What better place to rest than among those who permanently rested – or, so I thought.

The plums were delicious, enjoyed even more in the peace and quiet, as I leaned back, cradled by the protective ancestors about me. The coveted silence was short-lived. A squeak invaded my privacy. This was followed by a squeal that gradually grew louder, culminating in a crescendo which heralded the arrival of a venerable Chinese pushing a protesting wheelbarrow right through my lair. So much for seeking solitude in a land of millions.

Twice we were awarded passes to Chengdu, a large city twenty miles south of Kwanghan. We traveled in a 6 x 6 along a dirt road which led past the gate of Kwanghan and turned south, passing four large Pai Loos (arches) which spanned the old entrance road to Kwanghan. Halfway to our destination we passed the walled town of Sintu. The bustling city of Chengdu, which had long spread past its protective walls, now almost non-existent, boasted many universities staffed partly with foreign teachers.

A professor from Kansas invited two of us for dinner, and we enjoyed a home-cooked meal complete with persimmon pudding, although his wife must have blessed him for dragging us home unannounced. It was awkward for me to handle a dainty teacup after two years of eating like King Henry VIII.

Some impressions of Chengdu linger: a sizeable store whose only specialty was toothbrushes; a cloth maker whose purple-dyed material dried in festoons along the top of a remnant of the old town wall and the little university museum where I purchased a Ho Pu, an ancient coin of China made by Wang Mang in 9 AD.

The toilets in particular linger in my memory. They were nothing more than a gigantic cement pit brimming with watery excrement, over which was suspended planks with hand-holds for anyone brave enough to suspend himself over the pit for business reasons. In my haste to avail myself of the services of the pit, I slipped and narrowly averted a dip in the pool. (Which reminds me of a joke which takes place in hell and has to do with the devil meting out punishment. One individual is told to run down a hallway and dive into the pool at the end of the corridor. The guy runs down the hall and at the end he dives into the air, and as he arcs out over the pool, he can see people below standing in the pool with excrement up to their chins, their mouths barely above the surface. They're shouting as if with one voice, "don't make waves! don't make waves!") In the spirit of waste not, want not, the profit from the sale of Chengdu's excrement (which was used for fertilizer) supported the city's hospitals.

A GI by the name of Farrell was a stutterer. He went to Chengdu on a pass and ate upstairs in a Chinese restaurant. Having no money, he decided to go to the restroom on the ground floor with intentions of sneaking out without paying. The wily manager, however, was wise to the trick and waited outside the john with check in hand. Farrell emerged, saw that he was trapped and, resourceful GI that he was, yanked out a Colt 45, pointed it at the Chinese, shouted "Th-th-th this is a st-st-st-stick up!" and ran out the door into the night.

Mess (the eating kind) in China was cooked by the Chinese under American supervision. Pork slaughtered the night before, there being no refrigeration, and black-skinned chickens and sometimes duck, strangled hours before serving, constituted the meat menu, supplemented with garden vegetables. Once a week the Chinese would be given free hand to prepare the meal Chinese style, and these bring back pleasant memories. Eggs of any style were made to order for breakfast, and a cigarette bribe would encourage mess boys to make Kai M'imba (translation - fire bread, or toast).

A typical order would go something like this, "Hey, Joe" (all Chinese were called Joe -- what they called us was their own business), "Eggasa Wover 'n kao M'imba, Joe,"accompanied by a Chinese hand signal (one's hand waving under a piece of bread, denoting the fanning of flames). On busy days we might miss regular chow and have to settle for eggs. After many such occasions, one's appetite for eggs decreases, and after a day or two of eggs three times a day, other substitutes are sought after. During these times it was "K" rations to my rescue. The little cans of food were quite palatable, especially when I could get a mess boy to warm up the contents. Every incoming plane had a case of these rations on board so luckily there was a never-ending supply forthcoming.

Daily roll calls were non-existent in China. We stood only three during our entire stay at Hostel #3: on arrival day, and once -- for reasons known only to our leaders -- on a day designated for the testing of our gas masks. We answered the usual, "Here, sir," donned our masks and entered a tear-gas filled tent to check for malfunctions. This was the second and last time I would wear what proved to be the most unnecessary piece of excess baggage that we were obliged to tote. (Our rifle ranked a close second, followed by our helmet, whose only observed uses were as a wash basin, photo developing tank, and chamber pot.)

The gas mask test proved successful, unlike the first test back in the States, when the exhaust valve on my mask stuck open forcing me to grope my way out into the open air, blinded and gasping for air.

Another "success" concerned a single cavity discovered during a dental check-up. It was attacked with gusto by the dental technician using a drill that was mechanically turned with a pedal arrangement that the non-com specialist pumped up and down with his foot while he guided the drill into the cavity to ream it out. After he had finished packing in the filling, he was so proud of his accomplishment that he called his companions over to peer into my mouth at the finished product.

My Chinese American buddy, Lee, would frequently fly up to see me when his plane, "Lady Marge," flew up from India. Otherwise we corresponded via uncensored letters sent over the hump in the pocket of an obliging crewman. Normally, all correspondence was censored, sentences actually cut out making swiss cheese of our correspondence. My family never knew of any of my travels, but only that I was somewhere in China, for any hint of location, even enroute to our final destination, was judiciously cut out. We were allowed to send souvenirs home, however, and the censors would have died if they knew that the decorative Chinese characters written on them spelled out "Made in Kwanghan". (Translation courtesy of Lee.)

Operating a jeep equipped with a big sign on its rear reading "FOLLOW ME," I escorted a B-25 hospital plane to a parking place. They had come to pick up an armorer who had made the cardinal mistake of clearing a jammed caliber 50 machine gun with the backplate off and his face in the way. The gun discharged and the full force of the recoiling bolt, one pound of solid steel, hit him square in the face. No one heard anything more of this handsome sergeant, but then casualties were to be expected in our little game of war.

Actor Henry Greenstreet's son was in our outfit until he ran his vehicle off the road and was transferred to a rear base hospital and out of our small world in remote China. Speaking of actors, Pat O'Brien, and Jinx Falkenberg made it to China with a USO troupe, as did Ann Sheridan and Melvin Douglas. They had to off-limit one of the ten-holers for the ladies' convenience.

Two Red Cross girls made donuts in a shack down the road from the field. The sign hanging over the door spelled "Ma Foo Foo," the words actually meant "Horse Tiger Tiger," the Chinese way of saying "So-so". The delectables were passed out along with coffee to the grateful GIs working along the line. I was told that favors of a more intimate nature were also distributed to a select few.

Along about November word came through that a Japanese paratrooper attack was expected. In the days that followed, we started to dig in, making little forts around the field like kids playing soldiers. I was made a runner, supposedly to keep communications open between "fortifications." We had no ammo for our carbines, although I happened to have five rounds, and none of us had combat training so the picture looked pretty grim.

During this period, my friend Fitzgerald wangled a ride over the hump on a B-29 and we spent the day together while his ship was dropping bombs on Japan. The planes returned toward evening to be readied for their return trip to India the following morning. That night a three-ball alert was sounded, by-passing the one and two balls that generally preceded that final warning. I high tailed it to the cemetery with my precious five rounds and threw one into the chamber, as I crouched down in the darkness between the mounds of dead ancestors. The crew members manned the machine guns on the aircraft with orders to blow up the ships if and when the battle went against us. And so, we waited and...nothing happened! Next morning our planes flew back to India with a thankful Fitzgerald aboard.

On December 18th, our planes flew back over the

hump and bombed Hankow, China, the Jap staging-area field, knocking it out of commission. That supposedly put an end to the paratrooper affair.

Many of our planes were lost flying over the hump because of icing conditions as well as mechanical failures. One unlucky crew in the group had lost two planes and the crew had the "wind-up" and asked to be grounded, but the CO, Colonel Harvey, thought otherwise and convinced them to continue. They ferried gasoline to our field one day and as I was unloading our allotment, I spoke to one of the gunners about their problem. He told me in confidence that he was really scared and wished they would let him quit. Well, the plane headed back to India and was jinxed again. Orders came to bail out over India, and they started dropping out the bomb bay. As the crew chief was ready to go, his hat blew off, and he instinctively turned back to retrieve it. The guy behind him jumped in his place, landed in a river, and drowned, while the chief landed safely on the bank. The kid who drowned was the gunner who had spoken to me. They grounded the crew after that, but it was a little too late for him. Rumors spread that the kid had not drowned but had died of fright from a heart attack.

During our stay in China, more B-29s were lost due to operational failure than from enemy fire. The planes had no means of combating icing, and since severe icing conditions existed at certain altitudes over the hump, planes would ice up and lose control while passing through these altitudes. They learned that rapid ascent and descent through those areas minimized the accumulation of ice on the airfoil of the wings. The planes were better than their engines, and though they could fly successfully with only one engine, they could not take off with fewer than four that were fully operational.

One mission day, as we watched the planes roar one by one down the mile-and-a-half runway and lumber into the sky, one of our oldest planes, resplendent in old-fashioned camouflage colors, came into view at the end of the runway. It was struggling to get off the ground, one-wheel lifting, then dropping back, followed by the other wheel doing the same. Finally, in one last effort, both wheels cleared the ground with only one-hundred feet of runway left. It really lived up to the name painted on its nose, "My Assam Dragon." We had one other camouflaged plane, "Ding Hao" (Top Good). The rest were all shiny silver. Paint not only added weight but drag to the plane, taking 15 MPH off its flying speed. Later in the war, the bottoms of the planes were sprayed black to make searchlight surveillance more difficult for the enemy ack-ack gunners. Happily, another of our planes lived up to its name. "Hombicrismus" received orders to return to the States early in December.

Word came to us that Wyzola, the ocarina player who had entertained us in the middle of the Atlantic on board the Joseph Hollister, was killed while riding passenger on an ill-fated B-29 training mission. One plane, while on a mission to Japan, disintegrated after being hit in the bomb bay, and four smoking engines were all that could be seen falling on the Jap-held Chinese mainland below. Roy White, our barracks leader in Denver, bailed out at five hundred feet from a crippled plane going back to India and landed on his head, his chute opening just in time to save his life. One crew bailed out of a disabled B-29 on its way back from Japan. They landed in Communist-held Chinese territory, were walked through Jap territory to the Nationalist-held section and ransomed. From there they walked out, showing up back at A-3 three months after bailing out.

Having served six months in China, we were given a three-day pass for Calcutta, which meant a plane ride back to India to renew old acquaintances. The winter months in China had proven to be quite chilly, with temperatures dropping to freezing at night, so "summertime" in the winter of India seemed quite appealing. Furthermore, I was in need of a good shower, having foregone that pleasure for about a month due to the inconvenience of taking one in wintry China. My tent buddy Tex and I were finding the smell intolerable when we removed our shoes at night, so if for nothing else the benefit of a change of air would have been sufficient incentive for accepting the pass. It's nice to think it was the main reason, but truthfully, I don't think it ever entered into consideration.

We flew in a B-29, sitting on the floor of the rear pressurized compartment, and landed in India at Dudkhundi, our group having moved from Charra during my stay in China. The next day we trucked to Khargpur and took the train eighty miles east to Calcutta. We were billeted for three days in the Arabian College, a modern building which boasted flush toilets set in the floor to accommodate India's "sultans of squat". Tex refused to come, claiming no interest in any one town other than Wolfe City, Texas. "City," in this instance, was a misnomer if there ever was one. (When I dropped in to see Tex one day in the spring of 1947 while driving across the country with my mother and sister, I saw Wolfe City for myself -- a single street of half a dozen stores squat in the middle of an obscure section of farmland on the plains of Texas.)

Although Calcutta is a major metropolis, sacred cows wander freely throughout the city because no Hindu would dare to harm their reincarnated ancestors. Hindus are vegetarians for this reason, and some sects, like the Jains, wear cloth over their mouths lest they breathe in and destroy even the most minute insect. (After I returned to the States, I enjoyed having lunch with a Hindu and was surprised to see him eating meat. I asked him if it bothered him to be eating his own grandmother, and he laughingly replied, "No, here in NY, I'm probably eating yours!")

There were many homeless who slept on the

sidewalks at night, and at that time I never thought I'd ever see the same thing happening in New York City. The Red Cross ladies conducted tours, and Willets, Waranch and I joined them in visiting the museum, the mint and the ghats where Hindus were cremated on pyres of sandalwood. The ashes were then scattered on the waters of the Hooghly River, there to float by their bathing relatives.

One day we struck out through the off-limits back alleys of the native quarters. Deep in the passageways we were confronted by a Ghurka policeman who blocked our way. Strapped to his belt was a huge curved knife. He cautioned us to get out of there unless we wanted to end up with our throats cut for the little we had in our pockets. Needless to say, we took his advice. Incidentally, the Ghurka knife is used as a throwing weapon. One inquisitive GI asked a Ghurka to show him his knife. He obliged and then before sheathing the knife he cut the soldier's finger, a memorable way to learn that a knife drawn from its sheath must draw blood.

We had dinner one afternoon in the most fashionable hotel restaurant in the city, served by uniformed, turbaned waiters. The cost, a mere five rupees ($1.50). It was fun to ride in the open Ford touring cars (these taxis driven by turbaned Sikhs) or ride the rickshaws that filled the streets. The bazaars were lively with all sorts of items from jewelry to leather goods for sale. We visited one temple, leaving our shoes in the care of a boy outside, as we stocking-footed our way to the top of a minaret where the muezzin calls the faithful in the city below to their five periods of prayer each day. We dropped into the Jain Temple where a golden idol was being bathed in milk. We rode the tandem trolleys which never stop, only slow down, when taking on or discharging passengers. We thoroughly enjoyed ourselves even to the moment of departure when, in Victoria Station, I came across a bronze plaque set in the wall in honor of one Albert Edward

Fisher, which I deemed a fitting tribute to my father's memory.

On returning to Dudkhundi, we found that there was no immediate transportation back to China, so our vacation continued for another ten days until room could be found to ship us back to ATC aboard a C-46. We flew nonstop this time, over the glorious hump and back to A-3 where we quickly adjusted to winter, huddling around our tent's pot-bellied stove. Tex had converted it into an oil burner which consumed scrounged fuel -- used engine oil mixed with a little gasoline. It wasn't long before shoe removal became a harrowing experience once again!

The rigors of winter took its toll one night when an unfortunate Chinese soldier froze to death in his guardhouse. Next morning his stiff body was seen being carried away in (as one GI put it) "a sitting position of attention."

We remained in China until after the last mission in

January. Then one February morning after roll was called, we rode out to the field and boarded a B-29. After take-off, the pilot turned the plane and buzzed the field in a final salute to our home of nine months. Then climbing slowly up out of the valley, we headed back over the hump for India.

CHAPTER 6
BACK TO INDIA

Upon arrival in India, I was reassigned to the 677th squadron with no apparent duties to perform, since we were awaiting shipment to who knew where. We were billeted in a large stucco barracks with a thatched roof. Centered in the rafters was a giant oblong flat fan with a rope attached to it that fed through a hole in the end of the wall and hung to the ground below outside the barracks. Each barracks had a tent boy who received a half rupee (15 cents) from each of us each week, for which he would clean, make beds, collect laundry, and also pull the rope outside to fan the barracks' occupants. We slept on pallets; rope beds strung on simple cot frames. For another half rupee and a piece of GI brown soap, the boy would see that our individual laundry was washed in the river by the local women who beat it upon a rock until the dirt was pounded out, breaking most of the buttons in the process.

The English-style chow cooked by the Indians left a

lot to be desired. The bread always contained winged mites that had spent their shortened lives in the flour bin and their after-life in our intestines. We quickly learned to overlook their humble existence. Who knows? Maybe they contributed to the bread's flavor.

The women in India have a statuesque posture and strut like Madison Avenue models, the result of balancing heavy burdened water, dirt, or stone. The men are the diggers and loaders. When a basket is shoveled full, the digger and the bearer lift it up and place it on the woman's head, and off she saunters to dump it wherever it is needed. All these women, even the lowly street sweepers, the lowest caste, wear silver rings on their toes.

One day the order came to turn in galoshes. I don't remember ever wearing them, but I dutifully carried mine to the supply shack. Upon approaching the window, I could see the supply lieutenant and his sergeant loading boxes of clothes in preparation for our shipping out. His remark, "We better get some help in here," sped swiftly from my ears to my brain, prompting an instant fade away until a more propitious time to award him with my galoshes.

While we awaited shipment, with nothing to do, time hung very heavily on our hands. Mike Waranch and Willets suggested hitchhiking to Jamshedpur some eighty miles from Dudkhundi just for the hell of it. Timid Fitzgerald declined the offer, so we went AWOL without him. It was easy to hitch a ride thirty miles to Chakulia where the 40th Bomb Group was stationed, as there was frequent military traffic between the bases and the MPs were not checking passengers. We reached Chakulia in mid-afternoon where on subsequent inquiry we learned that the next fifty miles of our journey could be accomplished only one way. The morning ice truck was the sole GI vehicle that made a regular run to Jamshedpur. It was due to depart at 6 AM the following morning and we vowed to

133

be on it.

We hit the mess hall for supper, then found a vacant cot to catch some sleep. The next morning, we were at the motor pool and found the driver, a sergeant, who agreed to take us along. He and his helper rode in the cab and we hunkered down out of sight in the open truck, up behind the cab, nestled like stowaways amongst the straw in the bed of the truck. At the gate, the MP checked the driver for the necessary papers and waved him through. With his back turned as we drove past his station, he remained totally unaware of our existence.

The driver turned out to be a "Cowboy," calling upon most of the truck's horsepower to hurtle us towards Jamshedpur. We flew by a sizable town some twenty miles down the road, crossed a small river, then climbed into a low mountain range and twisted through its passages for the wildest imaginable next thirty miles. Fortified by a quart of gin, which the driver had purchased at a shack along our route, he haul-assed down that country dirt road with reckless abandon. On the outskirts of Jamshedpur, we stopped for a piss-call and then roared past the large Tatanagar Steel Mills and on into the city. We were dropped off with the instruction to be ready at 6 AM the following day for the ride back. I don't remember too much about that small city, but upon inquiry we were directed to a Red Cross billet where they put us up for the night, no questions asked. We ate in their canteen, relaxed around time, and generally killed time until we were ready to hit the sack.

The next morning dawned bright and clear, and as we arose we knew we had missed the truck's departure. "Not to worry," we thought, as we had breakfast. "We'll just hitch our way home." We walked to the outskirts of town and sure enough along came a British military lorry which stopped to pick us up. We jumped in back, joining six Ghurka soldiers and a tethered lamb, which seemed oblivious of its portending fate in the stew pot. We drove past the steel mill and took the single road out of town, headed for home, content with our good fortune.

Alas, our good fortune was short-lived. Ten miles out of town the lorry turned up a lane and dropped us off in the dust of our own company. There was nothing to do but walk the weary miles along the deserted main road in the hopes that some vehicle would pass and pick us up. Some five weary miles further along we passed a cut in the mountain where slabs of gray rock were being mined. Women were stacking them onto a truck bed. We were happy to see other humans in the midst of all that loneliness. However, the male foreman in charge soon dashed any hopes of an easy solution to our dilemma when he informed us that only one truck passed along the road each day. What else -- the ice truck that we had already missed! It was now past noon and we had fifteen miles to go before we would reach the town near the river.

Spending the night alone in the mountains was not something to which we looked forward. We sat down to rest, ate what food we had stashed in our pockets, then hit the long dusty trail again.

After half an hour we began to hear a faint noise -- the sound of some sort of transportation headed our way. Slowly a cloud of dust came into sight down the road, and as it grew in size, the cause of its existence appeared -- an Indian truck which was hauling coal. It squeaked to a halt at the sight of us -- three GIs frantically waving like marooned seafarers stranded on a desert island. Squatting atop the pile of coal were half a dozen native passengers, and we were allowed to join them. "What the hell, beggars can't be choosers," we thought, as the truck lurched forward and lumbered on its bumpy way toward our salvation in the town by the river some fifteen miles away.

We rolled into town about four o'clock, climbed down from our precarious perch, and promptly wangled a ride on a weapons carrier for the remaining twenty miles back to Chakulia. The two occupants of the vehicle were bearded "wild men," a pair of GIs out for a joy ride, stopping to take pot shots at any birds along the way, and thereby scaring an innocent maiden into high tailing it across a field while they shouted obscenities and laughed at her as she fled.

We arrived at Chakulia in time for mess, so we chowed down and then hit the sack, thankful that we weren't leopard bait somewhere up in the mountains. Next morning, we walked to the MP gate, gave the guard a handful of bananas, and asked about a ride to Dudkhundi, a calculated bold approach that paid off when he asked the next jeep driver coming off the base if he could take us to Dudkhundi.

Talk about good timing, we arrived back at our home base in time for lunch and as for good luck, no one in authority ever knew we had been AWOL for three days!

CHAPTER 7
ON THE MOVE AGAIN

Finally, in March, the order came to pack all gear and fall out on the road at 6 AM the following morning. We crammed everything we owned into our large duffle bags except for rifles, gas masks, helmets, and personal items, which we carried in our barracks bags and our small musette bags, which were slung on our shoulders.

The next morning, we fell out as ordered and sat on our gear to await the arrival of trucks, which we knew would be a long time in coming. Along about ten in the morning, a Captain with a couple of non-coms pulled up in a 6 x 6 and announced that there would be a showdown inspection for the purpose of finding purloined tools, supposedly spirited away by enterprising GIs. It seems that there were precious few tools left for the remaining crew chiefs and flying personnel to use servicing the planes which were relegated to remain behind during the period of our passage to our new theatre of operations.

Now everyone of us, including me, probably had a pair of pliers and a screwdriver, the two basic hand tools necessary for any service operation on an aircraft. To be subjected to a showdown inspection, which meant dumping everything we owned into the dusty road just to find a few measly tools seemed ludicrous to me.

As they slowly came up the road towards me, I noticed that they were searching each pile of belongings. After a pile was searched, the owner repacked his gear, shouldered his belongings and walked to a newly formed line of those GIs who already had passed inspection. Reluctant to give in to this insanity, I made no effort to unpack, waiting until the last moment to accede to their demands. As they started searching the guy next to me, their eyes riveted to his belongings, I saw my chance to just pick up my gear and calmly stroll to the newly formed line of inspected GIs. Needless to say, few tools were found. I saw one guy take a large bundle of tools out of his bag, big enough to choke an elephant, and hide it behind a tree until the inspection was over.

We loaded onto a Navy "K" Ship for another voyage to "somewhere," steaming out of Calcutta and anchoring down-river for the night, before proceeding eighty miles to the sea the following morning. At dusk someone shouted, "Fresh water in the showers!" Now if you have ever tried to wash yourself in salt water, you can appreciate what this rare aboard-ship opportunity for a good fresh-water soaping meant to us. I hot footed it down to the showers and really enjoyed soaping up and rinsing, letting the water cascade over my head, into my mouth and down over my body, not minding its slightly rusty coloring. Back up on deck, my fresh "Ivory feeling" rapidly left me as I gazed over the rail into the murky depths below and realized that I had been luxuriating in the shower under a geyser of Houghly River water which had been pumped into the ship's tanks in lieu of the normal ocean water at sea. As I looked upon the filth of that "Holy River," infiltrated with human ashes from the burning ghats upstream, the corpse of a dead cow slowly floated by in the murk below. Oh well, the Hindus consider the water to be pure and holy, and I must admit that I was none the worse for my ablutions.

My bunk was in the Canary Hold, a name given to the lower most deck, down at the water line, alongside the sweating steel plates on the starboard side of the ship. There were 2,500 men aboard with deck space for only three-quarters of that number, so that everyone could not be on deck at the same time, in spite of the empty top deck that was reserved for officers.

We sailed south into the Bay of Bengal and met another "K" troopship after which we were joined by two destroyers. The convoy traveled rapidly in zigzag fashion to avoid Jap submarines reported to have been off the coast of Ceylon. At sundown, all troops had to go below. As we proceeded farther south, the Canary Hold grew hotter and hotter until finally it hit 95 degrees every night when we went below. By morning it had cooled to a humid 80.

Navy chow was gourmet in comparison to army mess for this gourmand, who set sparks flying with knife and fork. Aboard ship I managed to augment the three squares with pilfered breakfast food, sugar, and cans of evaporated milk, as stacked along the side of the Canary Hold. One night an enterprising spelunker discovered an entrance into the cave below us, a storage-hold that was stacked with canned goods, some of which emerged nightly from the bowels of the ship supplying us with the mouth-watering goodness of succulent fruit salad. The piece de résistance was the ice cream served at mess, something the army was never capable of producing.

No one was allowed to venture within two feet of the rail lest some unwary GI fall overboard and be left as food for the sharks. To wile away the interminable hours between meals, we indulged ourselves with steel-deck poker or pinochle, or classic paperbacks from the ship's limited library.

Past Ceylon we parted company with the destroyers and the other troopship, and solitarily zigzagged our way south through the Indian Ocean. An albatross lazily crisscrossed our stern as it followed us for five days while we crossed the equator and sailed into the realm of the Southern Cross, which constellation appeared nightly, low on the southern horizon, advancing higher with each day of our progress southward.

Equator crossing is an exciting time for everyone aboard ship, particularly on a naval vessel. King Neptune reigns supreme and all pollywogs are forced to be initiated into the royal fraternity of shellbacks. Each captive is shaved, tarred, dragged into the presence of King Neptune to kiss his belly, and then slid down a chute into the dunking pool from which he emerges a begrimed, half-drowned shellback. All this is supposed to be good clean fun but in the confinement of a crowded troopship it borders on the ridiculous. I decided to lay low in an effort to avoid the roving gangs of seamen in search of their prey. I eluded capture all day. Late in the afternoon, I joined a card game on deck with some initiated shellbacks, carefully adjusting my hair under my cap to make it appear that I had been clipped. Fitzgerald also joined me and as we sat next to one another on deck, a roving gang came by and dragged off a protesting Fitzgerald, while I calmly proceeded to play poker, oblivious to his plaintive cries. The next day, when we received our shellback identification cards, I felt like a cheat, but at least a clean one.

After two weeks of zigzagging we rounded the southwestern tip of Australia, and with porpoises playing across our bow, we proceeded eastward across the southern waters of that continent to arrive days later in Tasman

Strait. We lay outside the city of Melbourne, awaiting the pilot boat, in a roller-coaster sea that tossed the ship up and down like a cork. A yacht-like craft approached, and the pilot came aboard to guide us to our berth inside the harbor.

We remained docked for one week, taking on provisions, oil, and water. The opportunity was given us for one day in town. A train took us into the heart of the city where I was surprised to see royal palms lining the main thoroughfare beneath which strolled the most pulchritudinous examples of fair maidenhood the likes of which had been denied my vision for almost a year.

I visited the War Memorial, set upon a hill a trolley's ride from town, and took in an amusement park in the evening, where I spied Duke, his long hillbilly knees sticking out of a Dodge-em bumper car. With his head thrown back he emitted guffaws of laughter, bumping his car around the arena, with the most beautiful blond Aussie gal seated by his side. When in Australia, one must partake of their delectables, one of which is steak and eggs. Having consumed two orders of that dish, it was time to settle the bill, in pounds, shillings and pence, no less. Well the system must have baffled the waitress, for I was able to show her the error of her ways when she tried to cheat me out of some coins of the realm.

The day had started on a sour note. I had come into town with Bernie, who upon arriving there informed me that he wanted his wrinkled sun-tans pressed. I couldn't care less about my appearance but went along with him to a tailor and waited while his pants and shirt were ironed. When he informed me that his next stop was to be a liquor store where he intended to buy some booze, proceed to a hotel, rent a room and lie in some cool sheets in a soft bed while he drank his bottle, I bid him a not-so-fond farewell, wondering why I had ever gotten involved with the creep in the first place.

When we finally left Melbourne, we sailed round

the eastern tip of the continent and north to the city of Brisbane where we took on some Aussie troops. From Brisbane our ship proceeded north inside the Great Barrier Reef through pale green sand-bottomed lagoons, the continent on the port side and the protruding reef on the starboard.

Leaving the reef through Flinder's Passage, we continued north, passing between islands off the eastern tip of New Guinea, rounding that promontory on Easter Sunday while attending mass on the top deck. There was a tense moment as the ship's automatic pilot steering mechanism went awry, and we were headed on a crash course for one of those islands. We proceeded along the north shore of New Guinea and put in at Madang, on a tropical lagoon with a jungle growing right down into the sea. The Aussie troops disembarked here. Some off duty Aussies were enjoying this paradise, sailing about the lagoons even as a buff-bare Aussie continually dove from the rigging of a small vessel anchored nearby, his private parts obeying the law of gravity as he descended into the water below.

From Madang a short passage took us to the Admiralties where we stopped at the island of Manus to pick up a handful of Navy personnel, whom we took further north to the atoll of Ulithi, a huge ring of coral reefs forming a natural harbor in the middle of the ocean. Ships were anchored in all directions awaiting the invasion of Okinawa.

We sailed northward from Ulithi. The Pacific was reduced to rolling swells on several occasions and remained truly pacific for our entire passage. In fact, Magellan, in his voyage of 1522, the first circumnavigation of the globe, encountered fair weather on every one of the 108 days that it took to cross the entire ocean. However, when he crossed the Coral Sea, it was just a couple of weeks after a storm had sent some naval vessels to Davy Jones's locker.

Conditions in the Canary Hold improved after a GI crawled up into the ventilation shaft and found the tube blocked with cardboard so that some wise-ass sailors could cool off their upper quarters at the expense of us sardines down below. Respite was to last for only the three remaining days of our voyage, for soon we passed the purple cliffs of Guam off our port side, then Rota and Agigan to come upon the island of Tinian in the Mariannas. It was to become our new home base. Forty-three days had elapsed since we left Calcutta.

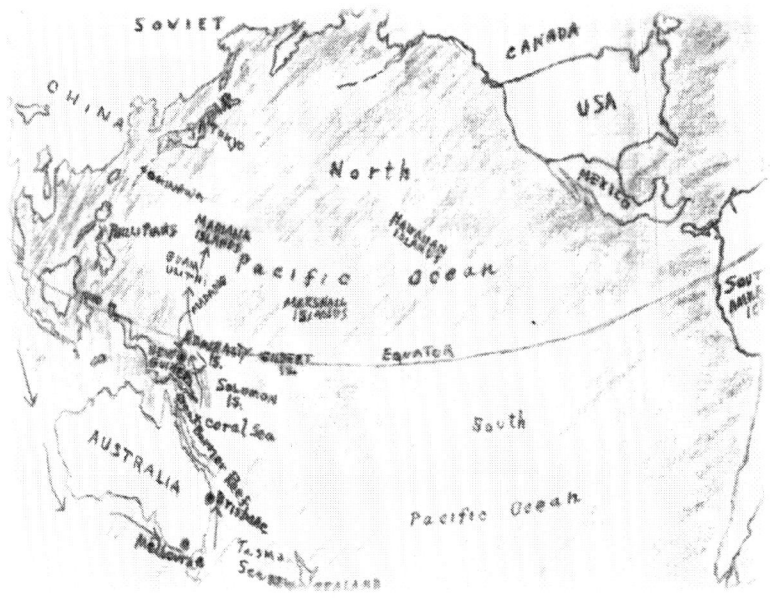

CHAPTER 8
ON THE ROCK

It was the beginning of May when we dropped anchor off the tiny man-made harbor of Tinian Town, nestled next to a small beach, which incidentally was the landfall of Admiral Anson on his voyage around the world in 1742. Landing craft came out to receive us as we scrambled down cargo nets and dropped into the boats with all but our duffle bags draped around our necks. The duffles were hoisted over the side and lightered ashore later.

The town, perched on a slight rise at harbor's edge, had been almost totally destroyed by U. S. Naval gunfire during the invasion of the island. Still standing, however, was a coral-rock pillar with part of its capital balanced atop, the last vestige of some primitive ancient civilization that had ceased to exist millenniums ago.

Tinian Island is seven miles long and three wide

roughly imitating the shape of Manhattan, its main roads bearing names equivalent to those on the New York island, such as Broadway and Eighth Avenue running north and south, with cross streets like 42nd Street and 86th Street. We were trucked to a sweet potato field on 86th Street, on what would be considered the west side.

A mess hall, administration buildings, a shower building, some 10 holers, and a water tank protruded from the center of an open area which would become our tent city. Until the tents were raised, we slept on the mess hall benches, but it was only a matter of days before row upon row of tents were ready to accommodate us.

Only a short time was needed to adjust to the routine in our new compound, a much shorter time to adjust to the routine to fit our individual fancies. For instance, the chow line could be observed from my cot, which made it convenient for me to stay in bed until the end of the line was entering the mess hall, when I could jump out of the sack, pull on my pants and shoes and race to the door before I was closed out. One had to be wary of being tapped for menial labor. This could be avoided by lying on one's sack with the orderly room door in full view so that any appearance of the first sergeant prompted immediate flight to points elsewhere. However, when it came to more formal work detail, occasionally one was outwitted and trapped, like the time volunteers were asked to step forward from the ranks, whereby they were rewarded with the day off, while non-volunteers like me were stuck with the task at hand. Is that justice, trickery, or both?

One day my name came up for rebuilding the coral walks that connected the tent areas. Well, it was shovel, shovel, shovel until I suggested to a fellow shoveler that we knock it off and dog it for a spell. Unfortunately, my remarks were overheard by an eavesdropping work detail captain. Needless to say, the next morning, on my day off, my name came up again for another day of detail shoveling. All day long I was goaded by that SOB captain, who kept asking me how I liked it. Somehow I resisted hitting him with a shovel! That evening I spoke to the first sergeant about losing my day off, and he gave me the next day off for my trouble. There's one thing I learned...you can't beat the system ALL of the time.

Trucks were provided to take us to the field, but usually I would miss them, being late to finish chow. So, I'd hitch a ride from any of the numerous trucks that always seemed to be on the move but would always stop for a fellow GI. If our plane was in, I would help service it, then lie in the shade under the wing until the truck picked me up for lunch. Back in our own area, we would eat and then truck on back to the line, nap some more until five o'clock when the truck would take us home. After a shower and chow, I might visit Fitzgerald in the adjoining tent area for a game of cribbage or visit Murphy and Lee in a third tent area for a gab session. To gain entrance to their abode, you knocked on the pate of a skull nailed to a post outside their tent. Some addleheaded GI had the foresight as well as the temerity to carry it all the way from India for just such a purpose.

On the southwestern tip of Tinian, the cliff drops down to a small sand beach. There the water is only thigh deep in pools atop a reef which juts out for seventy-five feet before plunging into the bottomless ocean below. The brave swam in the deep water. People like me merely bathed in the clear pools of water atop the reef. The pools were loaded with the most beautifully colored small tropical fish. They swam around our ankles as we carefully made our way along the sandy bottom, gingerly avoiding stepping on the six-inch spiny sea slugs that occasionally crawled across the bottom.

On a large coral boulder that rested on the shelf of the reef, a lifeguard shack had been erected to provide shelter for shark watchers, I suppose. There was no nude swimming, as the beach also provided respite for the members of the female persuasion, namely the Nurse Corps.

Much time was spent sightseeing the island or foraging for bananas or papayas that grew in isolated spots at sites of old farm buildings. During the process, a wary eye was cocked for any movement in the bush since Japs were still loose in the outlying areas. Sugar cane was the main crop on the island, which made it no problem at all for us to quench our thirst with the cool delectable juice of this succulent grass.

One sight to visit was Marpi Point and the suicide cliffs from which civilians plunged to their deaths during the mopping up operations rather than be taken alive by the Americans. The Japs had really put the fear of God into these poor people who were told to expect the worst if they fell into our hands. Nor did they heed advice from American loudspeakers exhorting them not to do the very thing they were doing.

One thrilling point of interest was on the southern end of Tinian. We motored to the top of this promontory, the highest elevation of the island. The road led to a grassy southern side. We wriggled up this slope to peer over the edge of a sheer cliff that dropped 584 feet to the ocean below. The whole island was nothing more than a solid chunk of coral thrust up from the ocean in stages to form roughly a two-tiered layer cake of purplish weathered coral. The ocean lapped at the lower layer while the upper layer was set back, with another ocean -- this one of sugar cane lying at its base.

Trade winds occasionally wafted pillows of clouds overhead, subjecting all below to short-lived deluges that refreshed the island's greenery as well as its inhabitants. There were no palm trees, all having been wiped out by land snails. The snails were brought in by the Japs for that purpose, in order to eliminate copra production in favor of sugar. When we traveled to the north end of the island, we could look across the three-mile channel that separated us from the island of Saipan. I remember seeing a straight line of dark clouds, an ominous weather front, stretched across the northern sky, hanging over the channel. Rolling down from the leading edge of the front were three spiraling cloud formations, one of which developed into a tornado that reached down to the water and traversed the channel in the form of a waterspout. It continued its course for perhaps five or ten minutes before slowly lifting up to finally disappear into the front of the clouds above.

Domestic goats roamed our living area, as did someone's pet mongoose. It and a young leopard had emigrated with us from India. The big cat was kept chained to the bulletin board outside the orderly room. One day a goat strayed close to the leopard. It sprang, snapping his neck chain in two. The shock dropped him to the ground short of his quarry. The big cat lay there in defeat, not realizing he had freed himself. Another time, while I was checking the bulletin board, I heard a growl emanating from beneath it. I was quick to heed the warning when I realized I was standing on the cat's tail.

The island was bird free, the recent hostilities having either killed or frightened them away. There were no flying insects either, but there were pesky little ants that invaded our beds at night and nipped us. We were forced to devise defensive moats by placing the feet of our cots in pans of water. Candy bars also had to be isolated on raised islands inside pans of water to discourage the ants' foraging habits, a trick they probably picked up from the occupants of the tent!

When the Officers Club was being constructed (some army, eh?) on a slope below our area, there was an instance of sniper fire directed at GIs on the roof. This prompted the marines to machine gun the Jap holdouts still at large on the island. We were forced to guard the camp at night to keep out unwanted guests. No Japs were reported shot or captured, but one interned native got lost and made the mistake of walking into an orderly room for help. He got a bullet in the leg courtesy of one scared first sergeant who opened fire in panic.

Here I was stationed on Tinian, not much more than a stone's throw away from where my brother was buried on the adjoining island of Saipan, just three miles across the water. (It was there on Saipan some twenty-five years after peace was declared that some Japs, who had been hiding out all that time, finally realized that the war was over, and turned themselves in.)

My application for a three-day pass to visit Saipan was granted, so I hitched a ride to the harbor and caught the daily ferry, an open LST, for the ocean voyage to our sister island to the north. Although only three miles of water separated the two islands, the trip entailed a passage of some twenty miles, taking me from the southernmost tip of

Tinian to Garapan harbor inside the reef midway on Saipan. We sailed north along the western shore of Tinian and Saipan to a break in the reef that allowed us entrance into the harbor.

Above us rose the 1,500-foot top of Mt. Topatchau. I hitched a ride to the B-29 field where I looked up a buddy of mine, Johnson, with whom I had been corresponding since Great Bend days. He found me an empty cot in his barracks where I slept for two nights, taking benefit of his mess during my stay, and enjoying his company and reminisces. Unfortunately, Johnson succumbed to a fatal disease after his discharge at the end of hostilities.

The next day I hitched a ride to the 27th Division cemetery and found myself standing helplessly in front of a plain white wooden cross. Nailed to it was one of my brother's dog tags. Across the road the water lapped a white sand beach which yielded unusual white shells as keepsakes of my visit. It was strange that George and I should meet on the other side of the globe at this remote spot, which had cost him his life in order to clear the way for his brother to follow.

George Justus Fisher, born in Brooklyn, New York, May 24, 1913, died on Saipan, Marianas Islands, July 19, 1944, age 31.

I snapped a picture of his resting place and after sent it home so that my mother and sister could also see it. After the war, Mom was notified that he was to be reinterred in the Punchbowl National Cemetery in Hawaii, but she elected to have his remains returned home and buried in the National Cemetery in Pinelawn, Long Island.

I spent the next day hitchhiking around the island on a sightseeing tour, circling the perimeter, and also jeeping up a steep road to the headquarters building atop Topatchau, then through the jungle on a lonely mountain road. The third day I caught the ferry back to Tinian.

Meanwhile, Gluck came back from a raid over

Japan and related how he had spared a downed Jap pilot's life when the Jap parachuted out of his plane and drifted into the sights of Gluck's tail guns. War may be hell, but heaven prevails!

A visit to the dentist became necessary when a gold inlay came loose and fell out of one of my teeth. I sat with other patients awaiting my turn in a shack reminiscent of a barber shop, the chair in full view of the suffering GIs, where the proceedings of the Captain of Dentistry could be followed by all concerned. The fellow ahead of me was suffering from a rotted molar which was diagnosed to come out. Novocain was needled into his gums and when dulling had commenced, the Doc took out a shiny stainless-steel cold chisel and a mallet and proceeded, with two forceful blows, to split the tooth into four parts, which were then easily removed with a pair of pliers. My job was easy -- just re-gluing my inlay -- but what about those other pain-wracked GIs awaiting their turn in the Captain's torture chamber?

Since our tents were pitched on sloping terrain, sudden rain squalls caused water to cascade down the hill and across the dirt floors of our tents. One night I stepped out of my bunk into a raging stream six inches deep. My GI compatriots got together and constructed a raised wooden floor from salvaged bomb crates, so that the deluge passed harmlessly under the floorboards. Speaking of tents, Gluck had quite a different problem in his. A large mound protruded above what should have been the normal level of the floor. In the process of its removal, they unearthed the body of a Jap soldier, who Gluck described as "some orderly room jockey with pencils in his pocket." The corpse was unceremoniously dragged across the road and dumped into an evergreen field nearby. Gluck may have had respect for the living, but precious little for the dead.

To harness the prevailing trade winds, some

enterprising GI constructed windmill washing machines to take care of the laundry problem. The wind would turn the fan which made a vertical rod move up and down. Inverted cups, which were attached to the base of the rod, were suspended in a wash basin below, in which they activated the suds and agitated the clothes in a soap and water mixture. This GI (meaning me) had no washing machine. He generally lived with what was issued to him. He built no floors or washing machines or storm doors. He converted no stoves to oil burners. (He did make himself an Adirondack chair from a bomb crate, copying a Fitzgerald prototype, but that was very uncharacteristic of him.) To him, washing was simple. For instance: (1) Do not wear underwear. (2) Do not wear a shirt. (3) Soak pants in gasoline. (4) Wash only socks, by the easy method of dropping them into a bucket of soap and water after four days' wear, adding another pair to the bucket every fourth day until the last of his four pairs had one days' wear left in them. Then it was time to swish the three pairs in the bucket, rinse them and then start a new cycle all over again. Two swishes a month was all that was needed to keep him well laundered. (NONE of this was learned at his mother's knee!)

In June, the powers that be temporarily reassigned me to a refueling outfit. The motor pool sergeant gave me a five minute "show me" crash course on the art of driving a 2,000-gallon gasoline tractor trailer. My job was to drive to the south end of Tinian, descend a mile-long road to the gasoline storage tanks, fill up my tanker, then crawl up the steep grade in "grandma low" gear to the plain above, and proceed to the field to distribute my load to thirsty B-29s. I befriended a fellow driver and we often traveled in pairs, racing each other down the taxi strips or sightseeing the island in our tractor trailer rigs. One day we detoured off the main road into what turned out to be a bomb dump, and in the process of maneuvering the rig, I backed off the coral road and came close to getting the truck stuck in the middle of nowhere, with no plausible explanation of why I would be delivering 2,000 gallons of gasoline to stacks of 500 lb. bombs.

At lunch time I'd steer my private craft to the mess hall of my old outfit to join my comrades for chow. While on assignment, I was able to maintain bunks in both compounds, as I could sleep or eat at either, and best of all, drew no KP at my new outfit -- my sergeant's stripes precluding such duties. In other words, it was the best of two worlds! Furthermore, my refueling "skills" were in demand only preceding raids. The rest of the time was my own. Alas, bliss finally came to an end in August when reassignment put me back in my old outfit, but in a different squadron, the 677th. And so, it was back to draining sumps and pulling plugs on another turd-bird, and back to disappearing from sight when the first sergeant emerged from the orderly room in quest of "volunteers" for some work detail. My ineligibility for duty with my old outfit was now gone with the wind. The old saying about "out with the old, in with the new" had just been reversed to "out with the new, and in with the old!"

One afternoon while awaiting the return of my plane, another B-29 made an attempt to land on the runway behind a small hill adjacent to our taxi strip. I heard the roar of an aborted landing as the pilot poured on the coals to try and take off again. He came up over the hill in a sharp turn, one engine smoking, the loss of its power causing him to veer sharply to the left as the full power on his right wing pulled him around. As it came in my direction, I vacated the premises, especially as there was a 4,000 lb. bomb resting on the ground next to me. As he turned away from me, my danger diminished, but his increased, for he couldn't hold up his left wing. It wavered downward, then upward and then suddenly dropped into the ground, which cartwheeled his nose directly into the ground in a sickening crunch of metal. The tail section remained pointing skyward for a brief moment, and then there was a whoosh as gasoline ignited in a ball of flame, the tail section falling into the conflagration below. As it burned, the shells in the gun barrels started to go off and whistle overhead as we ducked behind a vehicle for safety. Then the ammo in the turrets started to pop like firecrackers on the Fourth of July.

The plane burned furiously for hours, and when it burned itself out, the entire plane had been reduced to four blackened engines, two landing gear struts and a layer of white ash that delineated the shape of the fallen plane upon the ground. Oh yes, and one 100 lb. bomb. The plane was returning from a practice bombing mission, evidently with one bomb hung up in the bomb bay. When the pilot approached the runway on three engines, he was misaligned with the strip and made the fatal error of trying to take off with only three engines (a decision that was undoubtedly influenced by the hung-up bomb, which probably caused him to abandon any attempt to crash land the plane). That day fifteen men went up in a puff of smoke -- eleven crew men and four joy-riding sailors.

Our plane didn't have a good record, what with aborted missions and such. This was no fault of mine, considering the little they allowed me to do on the plane. Plugs were periodically changed on the four engines, which meant unscrewing 144 plugs from the cylinders and replacing them, all the while skinning knuckles on sharp fins in the process. We lowly mechanics were allowed to screw them back finger tight, the crew chief to follow with a special torque wrench to apply just the right pressure (eighty pounds) in tightening them. After he finished, we would button her up and she would be ready to fly.

Well, one time our plane took off after just such a procedure but was forced to jettison its bombs in the ocean and abort the mission when a loose plug was blown out of the engine and through the cowling. The crew chief had failed to tighten two plugs. On inspection, he quickly tightened the second one in a coverup, before it was noticed by the brass.

Maxwell, the guy who had mentioned his fear of attack, fell in with a GI and both of them became headhunters, scrounging through caves in search of the head of a Jap to be brought home as a souvenir. I don't know if Maxwell ever found his head. I do know that he met the fate he most feared. His plane fell victim to attack and was shot down in flames on a night raid over Tokyo.

The Chaplain shocked us at mass one day. He was speaking about the thoughtless use of vulgar language which seemed to constantly flow from the mouths of GIs. After we had entered the service, it wasn't long before some choice words entered our vocabulary. However, I had quickly realized that these little four-letter words were not necessary to convey a message. Any value that they may have had for emphasis was destroyed by their repetitive use.

One day I counted the number of times the "F" word was used in idle conversation between two or three GIs. Inside of two minutes the total came to forty. To illustrate his point, the Chaplain related how, on mission days, he and a companion Chaplain would stand in the operations shack and give absolution to repentant crew men as each plane rolled down the runway to take off on its mission to Japan. On one occasion, a plane aborted on takeoff and ended up in a ditch. The priests rushed to the accident, prepared to give any deserving casualty a free trip to heaven. As the priests approached the wreck they heard a frustrated crew man cry out, "God damn my fucking soul to hell!"

Now that I was back in my old outfit, my sergeant's rank got me no privileges, and so it was inevitable that the long arm of the KP pusher would reach out and grab me by the neck. KP was a six-day affair, from 5 AM until dark, with no time for rest. Besides cleaning the mess hall, we had to assist the cooks, serve the meals, prepare the vegetables, scrub the pots, dump the garbage, etc., etc. Peeling potatoes was a sight to behold. They'd put four or five of us on a pile of spuds and arm us with large chef's knives to chop our way through the slowly diminishing pile. The potatoes were cubed rather than peeled, the resulting garbage equaling the finished product. One evening, as we steered our weary bones towards the door, we were called back to shuck a pile of homegrown corn, little wormy ears, grown for us by the natives. We shucked until one wily GI figured out a way to shorten the ordeal. His plan was simply to fill each garbage pail three-quarters full of unshucked corn and top the pail with shucks. One guy hauled off a barrel of corn to feed his chickens. Needless to say, the job was finished in record time!

The thieving cooks were out for themselves in every

way. Out of the daily allotment of three small ice blocks which were meant to cool our beverages, one whole block was pirated for their own use. When we had chicken, a goodly portion would be stashed in the fridge for them between meal snacks, while late comers were served cold sausage in its stead. Once armed with this information, I never went short again. It was simple for me at any time to walk into the kitchen and go into the fridge for my fair share of their booty. You see, KP workers never wore shirts while we GIs were required to come to chow in them. Early on I had come down with prickly heat all over my back from my sweaty fatigues, so I dispensed with this burdensome apparel, never was challenged, and so could blend in with the authorized GIs working in the kitchen. When I needed lemons to make lemonade, which the cooks were too lazy to order made, I knew where to find them, and best of all, seconds on dessert were easily obtainable, freely bestowed upon anyone not wearing a shirt.

The army's most dreaded job, except for permanent latrine duty, was pots and pans. One toils the entire day in a steamy cement chamber with a garden hose for water and with a drain on the floor for waste. One was literally in the sink with grease-caked roasting pans and food-bedecked steam boilers, scraping, scouring, and steel wooling the stubborn grime into oblivion, with more water on oneself than in the pots. Custom dictated that two of the six days of KP were to be spent in this steam bath. Unfortunately, punishment for past sins caught up with me, for a third day was handed me on one sorry occasion. The army has a way of evening up the score.

One morning we were informed over the PA system that a powerful bomb had been dropped on Hiroshima with cataclysmic results. Two days later, on August 8, 1945, a second atomic bomb was dropped on Nagasaki and thoughts of an end to hostilities filled our minds. A week later, while seated on one of the ten holes allotted for a specific purpose (or should I say "end"), the loudspeakers announced that the war was over!

That night all hell broke loose, when GIs, crazy with happiness, started shooting off what ammunition they had for their weapons. I had already hit the sack before the fireworks started and was trying to doze off when an urgent announcement ordered us to turn in all weapons immediately. Well, I jumped out of bed, slipped on my shoes, grabbed my carbine, and dashed into the night, headed for the rapidly lengthening line forming outside the supply shack.

GIs quickly queued up behind me. As we slowly moved forward, I realized that I had forgotten one thing -- my pants. In my haste, I had rushed off, buff-bare, into the night. Not wishing to lose my enviable position in line, I reasoned that since we would file past the supply shack window, toss in our rifles, and then retire, it really didn't matter what I had or didn't have on. As we neared the shack, it became apparent that the normal routine of dealing through the window had been changed, for the window was closed. We wound toward the entrance to the shack and when my turn came, I mounted the steps, walked into the lighted room, crossed to the counter and, amid snickers from Captain and personnel, read off my rifle serial number, presented my rifle and walked out, to be swallowed up in the merciful darkness of the night.

Toward the close of the war, the U.S. warned the Japs of imminent danger to specific cities. Three cities were specified as possible targets for each succeeding raid, a sort of Russian roulette for the people of Japan to ponder upon each night when they went to bed. Even Hiroshima and Nagasaki were forewarned, but really where were all those people to go to escape the ravages of war?

It is a cruel fate that subjects civilians to the perils of war. Not only did the Hiroshima and Nagasaki bombings cause instant death to thousands of Japanese civilians, but the number of casualties in either of these two cities was surpassed on one windy night during the blanket firebombing of Tokyo, when that city was burned to the ground.

Missions over Japan continued, but they were missions of mercy. The B-29s dropped food and supplies to POW camps wherever our GIs had been imprisoned. These missions continued into September.

Sometime after hostilities ceased, the Mighty Mo, the battleship Missouri, anchored in Tokyo Bay for the signing of the peace treaty by General Douglas MacArthur and the Japanese. The B-29s planned a fly-by over the bay during ceremonies, and passengers were invited to accompany them on the flight. I would have jumped at the chance to go except that the day fell on our prescribed church day, equivalent to a Sunday, and I would have had to miss mass for the joy ride. I chose to go to church.

After the last atomic drop, word came down that the

two B-29s that dropped them had taken off from North Field on Tinian. We already knew of the 509th Composite Group at that field, who were dropping two types of bombs, known as Fatman and Big-Boy, but no one knew that these drops were a prelude to dropping the atomic bombs.

Fitzgerald and I hitched to the North Field and snapped pictures of ourselves standing in front of "Enola Gay" and "Bock's Ca." The latter plane had our squadron markings on it. The Composite Group had been using markings from all the different squadrons to mask its own existence from the Japanese.

About this time a typhoon (Pacific hurricane) hit the island and blew our tent down, so we moved into a newly constructed barracks and spent our remaining days on Tinian under a wooden roof, where many an all-night card game of nickel-dime was enjoyed.

Across the road from our area, a segregated Black construction outfit pulled out overnight leaving a motor pool of abandoned dump trucks. Soon GIs were sashaying around the island in their own private vehicles, but only for a short time. The brass halted these shenanigans by confiscating the trucks and having them deep-sixed off a cliff into the Pacific.

Bales of unopened clothing were burned in front of tattered native islanders who were prevented from salvaging some of it for their own use. My overcoat, which I had lugged three quarters of the way around the world, but only wore five nights in North Africa, was turned in and thrown into a tent full of discards to await cremation. I've often wondered what happened to all the broken birds of war, the B-29 wrecks that had been dragged to an airplane cemetery to be piled into an aluminum mountain, a gigantic monument to the god of war. On Saipan I had seen an entire quarry filled to the brim with the remains of vehicles, tanks, etc., lost by both sides during the invasion of the island.

In October we left Tinian by ferry for Saipan, to be billeted in a tent city on a slope overlooking Magicienne Bay, to await shipment back to the States. The central mountain range of purple-hued coral ran northward from our camp, which floated on a mound of coral above a sea of golden green sugarcane. I memorized the scene and made an oil painting of it a year after I got home. It hangs in my studio today.

My cot was in a tent on the edge of the embankment. In my haste to get to my bunk one day, I lost my footing, careened over my cot and flew out the open side of the tent, plummeting down the slope to end up in a cane field twenty feet below my tent.

For an entire month we waited for an available ship to take us home. We used to lie in our bunks and describe delicious meals, the likes of which had been denied us for the past three years. One day we were entertained by Barrett who described in side-splitting detail the way the medics had reconstructed his asshole.   One evening the island was rocked with a thunderous explosion when an ammunition dump blew up. Even this didn't interrupt the GI's thoughts of home and women for too long.   The standard question, "What's the first thing you're going to do when you get home?" drew the standard answer, "Well, the second thing I'm going to do is take off my shoes!" Some time was spent touring the island, a glorious way to cool off from the tropical heat. Standing bare-chested in the bed of an open truck was the way to blow perspiration to the winds.

I visited my brother again and offered a prayer as I stood by his grave in that peaceful setting for one final time. At a future date we would meet again when his body was brought home to be interred in Pinelawn cemetery with his buddies.

CHAPTER 9
THE FINAL LEG

We sailed from Tanapag Harbor about the first of December. They billeted me in the forecastle, way up in the brow of the ship, and as we headed into a rolling sea, my cabin started to yo-yo up and down like a seesaw. Lying in my bunk I could feel it dropping away from me, descending rapidly beneath me, then rising rapidly, it made contact again, pushing me up to start another cycle. My stomach started to rebel, and I headed for the open air and a spot amid ship where I clung to a stairwell for the next two days. On the third day my "sea legs" returned and after eating a good meal I was able to go back to the forecastle and ride the bucking bronco once again.

Our vessel was a Navy attack ship, with landing barges slung about the decks. At night we'd play cards in the game room, an empty chamber in the very stern. With every toss of the ship, the screw would rise partly out of the water, causing the whole rear of the vessel to vibrate, as we hunched over our game of steel-deck poker. Halfway across the Pacific, an eating accident cost me half a tooth, when I bit into a bone buried in a piece of pork chop. The tooth pained a little at night, so I reluctantly went to the shipboard dentist, an officer who serviced emergencies. He decided to temporarily slap some cement over the broken area until such time as I could get it repaired ashore. He dried the tooth in preparation for the application of the cement, which was applied and allowed to dry as I held my mouth open for what seemed like forever. When asked to close I complied. The plaster patch fell down onto my tongue and I can still hear the doctor utter that word of total frustration, "SHIT!" His second attempt at the repair job was successful.

Van Oosterom told the tale of being shot down off the coast of Japan, his B-29 ditching in the ocean. While the crew scrambled into a life raft, a sister B-29 circled overhead before flying back to the Marianas. As they floated alone in that vast sea, it became imperative that rationing of water and provisions take place. Impulsive Van Oosterom pulled out his colt 45 and threatened to shoot anyone who didn't adhere to the prescribed division of supplies. (He must have seen the movie!) Many hours later, the surface of the water was broken by an emerging U.S. submarine. When it became evident that they were saved, Van flung his pistol into the Pacific in wild relief. Patrolling subs off the coast of Japan saved many GIs in this dramatic fashion.

After two weeks at sea, pitching all the way home, we arrived at San Pedro, the port of Los Angeles. We were greeted by a band playing on the deck of the launch which accompanied us to the dock, where ladies passed out glasses of milk in lieu of champagne.

A steak dinner awaited us at camp, and as the damp winter air of a miserable day in LA penetrated our skins, overcoats were issued to us to shield our tropically tempered bodies from the cold. My first purchase was a half-gallon of ice cream, which, unfortunately, I just couldn't finish. I passed the last quarter of it to a friend.

After a few days' time they shipped us across the States toward home. I was assigned to share a lower berth with Barrett, the big guy with new "plumbing". Since I couldn't sleep with his big rebuilt butt shoved up against mine, I opted for a bench in the lavatory. Enroute we lost a few GIs who had detrained at one of the stops. They caught up with us in St. Louis. As we passed Wichita, Kansas, my encirclement of the globe was completed. I'd gone all around the world with Uncle Sam!

As we arrived at Crocker, Missouri, the train ground to a halt. This hamlet consisted of a small configuration of houses clustered upon the side of a hill near a half-dozen stores on what (with a stretch of the imagination) one might call Main Street. GIs jumped off the train, and as the delay continued, started to straggle up the hill to town. By the time the train showed signs of getting underway, half the GIs were scattered all over town. One GI stuck his head out a window of the train with, of all things, a trumpet in his hands, and proceeded to blow assembly. As the sound echoed off the hill, GIs started to stream back down the hill from all parts of town. They poured forth from stores and homes, clutching beer and provisions. The train waited until all were aboard.

We proceeded for about a mile and then lay up for the night. Come morning, behold beneath each car, an excremental stalagmite -- a pointed pinnacle of proliferation resting on the railroad bed underneath each toilet bowl of the train. Here was proof of the pudding (or whatever else we may have digested) that "all systems were go." The train proceeded slowly up the line and passed the cause of our delay on the previous day. A tangled mass of overturned boxcars was scattered about, cleared from the right-of-way during the night.

Our final destination was Fort Dix, New Jersey, where we were processed for discharge. We were given a physical and dental check-up, got our "ruptured duck" patch sewn on our uniform (three sides only of a four-sided patch -- for who knows what stupid reason) to prove to the world that we were civilians again. (I signed a waiver for that broken tooth so that there would be no delay waiting for some Army dentist to repair it.)

A bus took me to the Pennsylvania Railroad track where I entrained for Penn Station, changed to the good OLD LIRR and found myself back in Merrick, on the stoop of 24 Lincoln Blvd., waiting to greet Mom when she opened the door. I guess you could say it made our Christmas!

Indeed, I knew I was home when about two weeks into adjusting to civilian life, my mother started to come down hard on me to get out and get a job. My days in the 52-20 club lasted for only two or three payments before I was back at work at two-and-a-half times the salary I had been making three years before.

GI life was probably hated by all of us draftees, and most enlistees, and we were glad to sever our relations with the "disorganization." But retrospectively, it had proven to be a grand adventure -- one that this ex-GI is happy he did not miss.

- THE END –

LETTERS FROM OVERSEAS

Some letters from a collection dated March 1944-February 1945 by War Correspondent: Sgt Edward S. Fisher to his family

NORTH AFRICA-March 6, 1944

Are you surprised to hear from me here? Well, I'm surprised to be writing from this spot. Of course, I can't tell you exactly where I am, but for the time being we're living in tents on the open fields, and believe it or not, it's quite cold here at night and four blankets still leave us freezing. The days are warm enough when the sun is out. It's swell here, really picturesque and quite a lot like Van Gogh's pictures of southern France, with the exception that the peasants are Arabs, quite dirty, but quite picturesque, and the town is quite modern and old-world at the same time, and quite large.

I'll write a regular letter tomorrow and tell you all I can. The Mediterranean is calm and beautiful, and the Straits of Gibraltar were wonderful to see in the early morning light with Spain and the "Rock" on one side and Africa on the other. Land was welcome after 18 days at sea from Virginia without the sight of a grain of dirt.

March 7, 1944

I haven't gotten out of the camp yet, but I will soon, to get in some much-desired sightseeing and a taste of the wine that flows as water, and kicks like a mule. All around us are vineyards, but this being Spring, the vines are trimmed right down to the stumps, which make symmetrical rows across the brick red fields. Along the roads are rows of olive trees, and from our hill can be seen two separate towns, clusters of orange and salmon colored stucco houses wreathed with olive or cypress trees, their red tile roofs giving color to an already colorful landscape. Off in the distance are some large hills or mountains and the sky is lovely and clear and blue, with white tufts of clouds here and there. The sun is warm and the air cool.

In the fields one gets a flash of blue, yellow, or red and white, as the Arabs in picturesque costumes, tend to their fields behind their small horses. Although these latter are horses, they only stand about 11 hands high, or in other words, you can look right over their ears. They're ill fed, I'm afraid, and skinny, but are strong for all that. Then there are the burros trudging along the road with a seemingly giant of a man slouched on its back, with maybe a pack slung on either side of it also. Right across the road runs the little narrow gauge railroad with the funny little freight cars with four wheels, strung along behind two little panting engines that let out the shrillest of whistles, like air being squeaked out of a balloon. On the rear are one or two passenger cars.

When we docked, I was lucky enough to be left on board with some of the other fellows, to clean up our living quarters on the ship. We got to stay for two extra nights in the officers' quarters, and ate good chow with the crew, while our outfit was living in tents and eating canned rations and hard tack. We worked very little and had much time to spend in watching the Arabs or the (censored) unloading the boat. The Arabs were a riot in their baggy foreign breeches and turbans and their nomad moustaches using a strange gibberish speech and arguing with each other about how each thing should be moved. Their comedy nearly ended in tragedy several times, however, with narrow escapes from cables and hooks, etc. But what a time they had when, in lowering the baggage into barges, one of the duffle bags went overboard. In trying to fish it out, an Arab followed it into the water, and amid the noisiest bit of screaming and yelling of instructions in all languages, together with one man nearly being crowned with the derrick hook, and the bag sinking lower and lower into the water, they finally got a rope around it and pulled it out. (Yes, they pulled out the Arab, too). So, when we arrived in camp we only had to eat one meal of "C" rations, for we were changed to "B" rations, regular food in a scarce sort of way. But we were tipped off before leaving the boat and brought along quite a bit of crackers and canned goods to augment the small rations here. At night before bed, we have cocoa, etc., thanks to the ship's supplies, but we keep saying, "If we only knew sooner, before they locked everything up." We only got away with a one-gallon can without a label (we're saving it for a surprise) 5 cans of milk, 3 boxes of corn flakes, 6 dozen cookies, 6 cans tomato paste, 5 lbs. of cocoa, 3 lbs. of sugar and 5 oranges.

March 9, 1944

We visited an abandoned farm next to camp and picked up some fossils of seashells embedded in stones. The buildings were in ruin, roofless, with crumbly walls, with little oblong slits for windows, an abandoned well, etc. The houses are made of the pink and orange stones from the field and are put together with crude cement or clay, and are very picturesque, in ruin or not, with the olive or cypress trees around them, and with the fields of red dirt fading into the hills and mountains in the distance.

The native (Arabs) are quite shabby looking, due they say, to the scarcity of clothing and the reluctance of the authorities to sell them anything. A colored boy who has been here a few months told me that he has already been offered the equivalent of $20 -- for a bar of soap -- from a raggy Arab with a roll of bills. However, if one is caught profiteering this way by selling GI equipment or otherwise, the punishment is steep. The fellows got some chalk and marked all the tents with different names of hotels and such. Probably the cleverest was the inscription "Frank Sinatra slept here -- Swoon!"

INDIA - April 20, 1944

Dawn has come up over the rice fields and has turned India into a wonderland of beauty and enchantment. I wish all of you could have seen it in the half-light before the sun came into view.

I tumbled out of bed in a twilight myself, and in between rubs to banish the remaining tears of sleep from my eyes, I could see a grove of trees all around me, an aviary of hawks, crows and birds of other description, identified only by too whoos and other bird gibberish. There was only coolness in beautiful respite from the heat of day that was to come. An occasional cow cropped the stubble of last year's rice harvest aimlessly wandering between the thatch-roofed houses. This then, was India early in the morning.
In the afternoon, it will be different, for the sun will blaze down unmercifully, and, as the song goes, only mad dogs

and Englishmen (and a few Americans) will go out in the midday sun. Harking back to the days in North Africa -- Yes! The Arabs speak a sort of French but it's difficult (impossible for me) to understand any spoken French and their gibberish was unintelligible. They could understand French or Spanish, but I didn't try to speak, for I've forgotten most of it already.

Let me tell you about the ceremonial dances we saw. Down the street came a maharajah sitting cross-legged on a flat cane mat suspended from a bamboo pole, which was being carried by two black footmen. Leading the small parade were four or five drummers in fancy dress, colored in reds and greens, with bells (like sleigh bells) around their ankles and waists, beating out a jungle-like rhythm on drums decked with deer antlers. Behind on foot followed some women, probably servants. It was a small affair, not lavish, and obviously he was just a small-time maharajah.

Well, the entourage had to stop and wait for a train to get out of the way (even maharajahs have to suffer this indignity) and so while his nibs squatted under a shade tree with his servants (or wives), his circus drummers cavorted to the delight of the soldiery, thus relining their own pockets at the same time with rupee notes, and as may be expected, a good time was had by all. They had some ritualistic dances on the program (all properly arranged by an overseer in a blue coat who took his cut of the money) and somersaulted and gyrated the while they beat weird melodies from their rattle-trap drums. They looked fierce, one looking about two shades lower than a low-grade moron, but it was colorful to watch.

We haven't seen any cobras or elephants or tigers as yet, but one boy reached his hand into a bag for a bar of soap and out crawled a scorpion. The latter was as surprised as he, and in the excitement the scorpion lost his life. Our barracks here are quite roomy and cool, being built of cement and brick, and with a straw-thatched roof, housing birds and lizards as well. The latter come as long as a foot and a half. You should see the hawks down at the mess hall when we eat chow. Between 75 and a 100 sometimes circle overhead, and since each one measures three-feet across the wings, you can imagine the confusion, especially when they swoop down and pick up food with their talons, sometimes even taking it right out of some unwary soldier's mess kit to his chagrin and everyone's amusement. They also catch morsels thrown into the air in the same way.

SOMEWHERE IN CHINA - May 4, 1944

Well, I guess I never will get settled in one place for long. Here I am right next door to the land of the rising sun. You're never probably thinking to yourselves, "What a place to land in," but you are as wrong as I was, for this is a nice country and the people are the friendliest in the world, and get a great kick out of us, as we do from them. You'd be surprised how well you can get along conversing with your hands. They pick up English very rapidly and I wish I could pick up their language as fast.

Yesterday some Chinese soldiers were trying to teach me how to speak, pointing to objects, and pronouncing them. I don't know how. I got a few of them, but some were real tongue twisters and a gathering of about ten of them got quite a kick out of my antics. (One of them is peering over my shoulder as I write this, watching the pen fly). They really are the happiest people I've ever seen, and for Chinese supposedly being unemotional, I disagree, for they are quite natural, and always ready to laugh. They had a good time helping me to use their shower, and when the sprinkler fell out of the bucket overhead and water poured out, while I floundered about to put it back in place, they split their sides.

The food is the most excellent I've eaten in a year and a half, served to us at tables with tablecloths. You see, we are guests of the Chinese government, and they feed and take care of us, cook, and wash our clothes, etc. This is the best spot I've had since the draft caught me. The work is hard and long, but the living conditions make up for it, and anyway, I'm only too glad to work hard now that we're somewhere where every effort counts towards a specific objective.

This certainly is the land of the rice paddy, with rice growing in all different stages, being sprouts in one field, and harvest in another. I've eaten all kinds of strange vegetables, all of which are delicious, and most every meal is like dining out in a Chinese restaurant.

I'd best not speak about how I came into China but will leave it to your imagination. It was an experience I'll never forget. Pay day when it comes will bring me about $13,000 in Chinese money, the equivalent of about $60 American for two months' pay. I'll need a bushel basket to carry it, for the largest denomination is $200 -- equivalent to $1 American approximately.

May 9, 1944

It looks awfully curious to see a huge water buffalo, up to its neck in water, pulling a submerged harrow, and a partly submerged Chinaman, up and down a rice paddy. The water is about a foot and a half deep and the mud another foot, but the buffalo weigh so much that they sink more than half-way in. These animals are huge and stand as high as these small Chinese and weigh twice that of a cow. The water wheels are also picturesque. They are flimsy bamboo constructions over which is a sunshade. Under this two Chinese sit and pedal a wheel with their feet which in turn is geared to a conveyor belt with buckets, which transport the water up and over the paddy walls. Very often you see ducks swimming on the paddy surface, and local nimrods cast their lines into the water to fish out tiny perch at the end of ponderous bamboo poles.

The village stores and tea rooms along the road are quite unlike the Barbizon Plaza, although the sidewalk tables are quite similar. The Barbizon doesn't have little black pigs tied fast to a tree growing alongside, digging and grunting, nor do they have the latrine as close to the tables. The only thing about India that I miss are the beautiful skies.

I've never seen anything like them, and though each was different, one was more beautiful than the other. Up until I arrived in India, I was under the impression that in spite of what people said, all skies were of the same beauty. Speaking of skies, it's fun to fly over the clouds, so that all is just like the misty carpet of heaven (as depicted in "Here Comes Mr. Jordan" some time ago) and then to come to a cottony thunderhead thrust through the floor of the sky and rising in a brilliant blaze of sunlight. They look just as they do from the ground, but I've never come so close to reaching out and touching one, almost four miles out in space.

This is the next night and I just had me a sip of good wine which costs $400 a bottle ($2 American). Now to continue. Yes, this is the land of big hats and bound feet. The women plod along the road, plop, plop, plopping their immature size fours like horses clopping down their hooves, for little else are their bound feet but hoofs, sans arch or form. The people always give us the thumbs-up sign and shout their version of "Hello" as we ride by. The thumbs up means that they approve of us as Ting Haow, or good.

You ask where I was in North Africa. The place was Oran in Algeria, about 250 miles from Tunis, I believe. I was driving the big 10-wheel truck yesterday, and later took the boys to chow in the smaller one. They thought they'd never make it, and I had my doubts two or three times. You drive on the left side here and that right side of the truck was nudging those Chinese carts off the road. Oh, well! We made it, and that's the main thing, although the boys sitting on the fender were ready to bail out at any moment.

June 28, 1944

I'll tell you a little bit about the walled city near where we are stationed. Like all traditional Chinese cities, it is entered through an iron-studded gate set into a deep high wall, whose battlemented sides curve off to both sides, encircling the city. How old the wall is, I do not know, but surely it must be as old as the town, and since this is China, the town must be very old. There are four or five gates to the city, over each of which is a watch tower with a fancy upturned oriental roof, a large bronze bell, and some Chinese soldiers. From the outside, the wall is about 25 feet high, but inside the ground is slanted up to the battlements, through which the soldiers of old launched their arrows. At one point a block house is built out from the wall, down into which the soldiers could climb to command a view of the wall from ground level through slots in the block-house wall.

Inside, the city is a crisscross of dirty, dusty streets walled on both sides by stores, one and sometimes two stories high, so that, as one soldier aptly put it, "The whole town is nothing but one continuous building." Going down any normal street one may encounter any or all of the following -- rickshaws pushing by through the people; the ever-screeching wheelbarrows loaded with grain or bamboo, or large carts pushed by six men, elbowing through the crowd, occasionally an alcohol-fueled Chinese truck scattering everything right and left (everything and everybody uses the road -- the so-called side walk is approximately two-feet wide); there's a pig or two or three being driven to market by a Chinese with a stick, past two or three dogs lolling in the dust; pullets and chickens and little nude children scamper by; there's a mother nursing one of the 400 million; over to the right an American soldier is at a store buying a bottle of wine and there are about 25 Chinese gathered around in a circle, filling half the street; hold your nose, we're passing one of those open air latrines;

there's a poor leper sitting on the curb, seemingly waiting to die -- look away quick or it will turn your stomach; over here is the candy store -- let's buy some peanut brittle -- $100 worth will be enough, about a pound; now we pass a meat store with half a pig hanging in the dust and foul air, over there are dried chickens for sale; or old green-mold aged eggs, a delicacy; smell the odor from the tea room; such a variety of smells, so strange, so oriental, so obnoxious, most of them -- what we need is air -- ah! -- here is the north gate that leads out into the country again; let's get a little fresh air before we go back through the city gate again. And so, refreshed, we go back, but this time we skirt the streets and go around through the park, and the improvement is tremendous.

We stop to look at some statuary, strange monuments to stranger deities, set up at one point in the park, and thus after emerging into the city, getting lost and finally coming across two soldiers who set us right, out we go to hire a rickshaw and bump back over the road at a dog trot for several miles. Here we are, back at the hostel -- what's the fare? $70. Oh, give him $100 and a cigarette for a tip. He earned it!

This I hope gives you a little insight into our life here in China. It's a good life -- a little monotonous at times -- but oh! so much better than a foxhole. Enclosed you will find $100 for a souvenir. (Don't spend it all in one place!) It's worth approximately 50¢.

You ask if there are flowers here. No, there aren't, but one doesn't miss them here somehow, for they hadn't occurred to me until you mentioned them. However, one can't expect them here where every bit of land is under cultivation (99% of it rice) excepting the fields of mounds (graveyards) which come to think of it could have flowers, but somehow just don't. Everything is green here, and that's all. The farmhouses and barns and outbuildings are clustered like little islands in the fields and always have a mud wall completely surrounding the whole unit, through which one enters by a wooden door set in one side. In Africa, like in France, the same holds true, excepting that the walls are of orange brick. Here houses, walls, etc., are built of bamboo, straw, or mud bricks.

So, you have me speaking Chinese by now. Well, you can forget that right now. We can say a few words once in a while, but when one sound can have five to seven different pitches, and each pitch can mean more than one thing, how could anyone learn how to speak it? You could hear one sound and it could have as many as twenty or thirty meanings to an untrained ear.

About bound feet -- the poor as well as the rich bind the women's feet -- (that is, if the rich do it -- I've never seen a rich Chinese here). The younger generation, however, are not bound and I imagine the middle aged and older women we see hobbling along the road are about the last ones to ever practice that timeless custom.

August 7, 1944

Well, yesterday I got the day off, and transportation to the nearest Chinese city, forty miles away. We went by truck over the dusty, bumpy roads and the two-hour ride was quite an ordeal. But the experience was well worth the effort, for our primary objective was achieved. We had what we went after. Our first ice cream in nearly six months, our first cold drink (with ice) in over three. Well, we made pigs of ourselves, of course. Whoever heard of having two plates of ice cream and a cold drink as an appetizer for a meal, but that's what we had. Anyway, at the end of the day, the score was eight plates of ice cream and eight cold drinks at $80 and $70 apiece, respectively. (40¢ and 35¢ American). The ice cream was the size of a nickel scoop and half sherbet and half ice cream at that, but what cared we for price or quality -- it was cold, and banana flavored! We also stopped in at the high-priced place -- paid $165 for a cold drink and $150 for the same size ice cream. (Two of us spent $5 American in there in five minutes). The total cost for me for ice cream and cold drinks for the day: $7.50 American.

But, something about the city. The main streets are wide and teeming with dashing rickshaws, occasional Buicks, and Fords. This is the cultural center of China for the present, and no less than five (censored) are housed here. The sidewalks are wide enough to walk four or five breasts, are lined with trees that someday will offer shade if they can thrive and grow in all the dust.

The best streets have the eastern version of the modern store lining the way, and some of these stores are quite modern and surprisingly clean and neat, especially to our eyes, so used to filthy, little Chinese towns. The city abounds in jewelry shops, with innumerable clocks and watches for sale at prohibitive prices (i.e. a watch, American make, worth about $150 American -- price $165,000 or $850 American). Soap -- Lux $1.20 American a cake -- get the idea of prohibitive prices? -- American cigarettes -- $12 American a carton!

The people here with a little money have privately owned rickshaws, so like a Victorian carriage in comparison to the "Model T" rickshaws for hire. And the propelling power, the human horse, the coolie, sets quite a pace through the streets, clanging bells to make headway through the congestion.

We saw nothing of cultural interest, being obsessed with only one idea, that of refreshment. The city is walled, as are all Chinese cities and towns, but the entrance gate is gone, and the wall is cleared back fifty feet on each side at the entrances to the city. The usefulness of the walls is practically gone, and thus with these alterations go some of the city's charm. One hardly notices the wall at all as one enters the city, very unlike the town near here where one passes through a dark archway between iron-studded doors to gain admittance.

To say the Chinese are different in a large city would be foolish, for the Chinese seem to be the same everywhere, of course, a higher class of people are seen in the larger cities, and they have a more modern outlook on life, but China and the coolie are synonymous, and where there is one there will always be the other.

August 11, 1944

You said it! Chinese is hard to learn. We always have a lot

of fun with the Chinese boys up at the mess tent on the line. They always tell us the Chinese pronunciation for things, and we tell them the American. I must say, they catch on much faster than we do. Their sounds are so alike that one forgets them quite easily. I heard one of the waiters singing "Oh Susanna" the other day. He picked it up from the mess sergeant. We tried to straighten him out on some of the words, but he had to give up after a while, so we rendered a three-part harmony for him, and the lesson ended. Know your mess boys, I always say, for they control the grub! A few cigarettes handed to the right boy ensures friendship and, incidentally, seconds on sweets!

I managed to get hold of a small can of Spam the other day and thought it might augment my tiresome diet of eggs for breakfast so I hurried myself to the mess tent, sliced the Spam on a plate, and one of the mess boys placed it on the stove so the cook could fry it. I could see it sizzling in the plate as it got warm and my mouth started to water (imagine one's mouthwatering for Spam!). The cook reached over for the plate, picked it up, howled and his burned fingers released Spam (lovely, sizzling slices) and plate in mid-air, and Spam scattered all over the mess tent floor. Result, eggs again for breakfast!

Ugh! What I wouldn't give for a cold heaping dish of cornflakes! We have pancakes quite often now, though, and they are really quite good.

August 15, 1944

China is about the same. The rice is well along, and coming to a head, turning brownish, and will soon be ready for harvest, the second for this year. It looks rich and soon the grain will be bursting through. The weather is moderately hot, but not nearly as bad as July, which is the hot month in this locality. The Chinese are still as friendly as ever, and much richer since the Americans arrived. Prices are fabulous and the rickshaw rates have more than tripled in some instances.

The Chinese are very honorable, and although graft, and their "squeeze" are quite accepted, stealing is punishable by death. And thus, our valuables are safe as far as they are concerned. It's the GIs themselves who spoil things sometimes, for there's always one in every bunch. Occasionally there is a Chinese, too, for one was caught the other day.

They are very curious and will gather 'round and gape for no reason at all. I was reading your letter out in the rice fields on the way to work, and stopped by their irrigation system, a sort of busy little waterfall. It didn't take long for a youngster to sidle up and peer over my shoulder, so I handed him one sheet to read. He took it, peered at it as if he were reading it, then handed it back and gave me the ever quoted "Ding How" (top good!). Everything American is top good, except perhaps the food we eat which is strictly "Boo How" (not good), for to them, sweet pork and rice and their peculiar vegetables make up the right sort of diet.

You speak about ice and refrigeration and ask how they keep things fresh and in good condition. The answer is that we get all our food freshly killed or picked. The pigs are probably butchered the day before, the chickens and ducks meet their executioner behind the mess hall, the vegetables are brought in fresh picked, and the eggs ("pronounced egg-a-ses" in Chinese American) are freshly laid. Ice is unheard of here, and the only refrigerator is one in the hospital. One sees the pork hanging in the marketplace in the dust and the heat, or on a hook being carried along the road. I don't know how it keeps from turning. You should see the dried chickens and ducks they sell, or the dried killies (these little fish from the irrigation ditches), dried ray fish (those flat ocean fish).

The chickens are plucked and cleaned but are flattened out, head and all, and dried to a grotesque, shiny, red dish, nightmarish object. But you should see the moldy eggs, old and gray -- a delicacy they tell me. Enough about food.

Speaking about fruit, as you were, we can now obtain luscious red persimmons, as well as pears and a type of date. They also have a strange looking grapefruit with a green skin of an inch thickness. It is rather bitter and dry inside.

August 27, 1944

The other day we went into the foothills of the mountains nearby. We had to go over that way and travelled the first 4 miles in a weapons' carrier. Then we started walking and in a mile and a half we came to a river which was too wide to cross any other way but boat. We took a sampan across about three blocks of water and waded ashore on the other side. After that, it was a good 5 miles over roadless country, winding through cornfield and sugar cane patches to our destination. The country is nice up that way and there is very little rice grown there.

On the way back we refreshed ourselves in two ways, by eating sugar cane to quench our thirst, and by submerging our steaming feet in the irrigation ditches, shoes, and all. Along the river we passed some unusual caves of red sandstone with carvings of figures on the walls. It probably was some sort of altar or place of worship, and as we didn't have time, we left it unexplored. The sampans are just like they are in the pictures you've seen, long low boats with a curved mat in the center as a form of house. They have about 6 inches of water in the bottom and are full of mosquitoes, which breed right in the bottom of the boat.

I'll enclose the negative of my picture in this letter for you to do with as you see fit. I thought it was a rather good picture of me, although it probably looked strange to you, who wouldn't recognize the new edition of me with my new addition. I gave birth to it on the boat, have never shaved the old lip since leaving the States, and won't until I hit the home shore again. It has led to many nicknames over here. All the Chinese call me "Fou-za" which, of course, means moustache. Then there are the boys who call me Teddy, derived after we all saw the movie "Arsenic and Old Lace," from the character of the crazy brother who thought he was the first President Roosevelt. They also call me Mr. President. Then there is the faction that still calls me E. Southworth, and other minor allusions class me as Buffalo Bill, and Groucho Marx. Indeed, the names change as does the shape of the moustache.

September 2, 1944

One thing about these Chinese, they are traditionally always knocking their own and boosting the American product, and they will argue with you in a stream of Ding Hows and Boo Hows if you mention that something American is Boo How (not good). They get a kick out of trying to write English, and love to compare their symbols to our words. Right now, there are five *of* them going over the business of names with Tex, writing right and left bilingually. They've just concluded now, and one just said, quote, "Ding Boo How," which, combined, means Top Not Good, or very bad.

Well, I just got my pen back from one of the Chinese who have descended on us again. We've just settled that we'll have a movie tomorrow. They love to go and see them although I don't know how they understand what they are all about. Now we've just settled the financial situation. I'd better close and get out of here before we settle world affairs.

September 15, 1944

This is the season for harvesting the huge rice crop that bends its laden stalks in a golden sea of grain. Already, here and there a field appears with rows of straw stacks where the farmers have waded in and started to clear, thrash, and stack, a task seemingly comparable to bailing out the China Sea with a bucket. As the green rice used to be beautiful against the purple mountains, so now the gold.

We went to town recently and stopped in a small cubbyhole of a shop to watch a young boy of ten run a loom, using both hands and both feet in a coordinated action that really turned out the cotton cloth. The machine is very simply constructed and was manipulated with jerking and stomping in a noisy rhythm of moving wood against wood, with the slap of the shuttle clear above the din. Outside on the sidewalk, a man and woman were spinning the thread and winding it on spools to be used inside on the loom. Around the corner, another shop was running a machine to fluff up the cotton bolls into fleece cotton sheets, from which rolls are made to put on the spinning wheel to make thread. And, of course, to complete the picture, we passed the growing cotton on the way into town.

The boys start to work at what I would approximate as the age of 7 or 8 years, and you see them helping their fathers to pull a screeching wheelbarrow along a bumpy road. By the time they are about 10 or 12, they are on full time, working along with the men, pulling carts, mending roads, carting dirt, etc. You should have seen how proud the loom boy was as we watched him doing a man's work.

The article Gin sent me about the coolies and the heavy carts they pull is accurate. Although we don't have hills right here, the wagons are loaded to capacity for even ground, and even a slight rise in the road gives them trouble. I understand that coolie means "bitter strength" in Chinese, and the name couldn't be better affixed.

On the way from town, I've come two and a half miles by rickshaw, the boy dog trotting all the way. Although the road grades very slightly downward coming from town in good stretches, imagine someone pulling a hulk like me, and running on top of it. Yet you can go to the city by rickshaw, a distance of 30 miles. One big boy here (about 250 lbs.) exaggerated when he said that when he sat down in the seat, he lifted the coolie right off the ground, his feet paddling in thin air. All rickshaw coolies must dub Megways (Americans) as Pon-za (fat)!

The farmers with their wheelbarrows push a tremendous load also, trucking their goods to town. But do you think they are content to come back empty-barrowed and rest a little? No! They have a sliding back that they insert into the barrow and they truck passengers back in this improvised seat.

You should see their waterpipes (for smoking). They are small enough so that one holds it in the hand. It's made of metal and has a compartment for water and a stem leading from this. Then there is a long narrow bowl (like another stem) coming up on the other side. Into this is inserted a pinch of tobacco from another compartment with a tweezer that reposes in a slot, when not in use, along with a brush for cleaning purposes. Then the tobacco is ignited with a piece of punk and inhaled in one big puff of enjoyment. Then it's pftt! -- blow out the old ashes and start all over again. (In other words when you smoke one of those, you smoke, and smoke only.) But they have plenty of time over here for this -- centuries.

Saw something -- two GIS travelling in rickshaws and as they neared their destination, one said to the other -- "Now?" The other answered, "Now!" and they both got out, changed places with their coolies, and steam-rollered down the road to their destination, with two beaming coolies "ding howing" all the way.

I've been trying to get time so that I can learn how to play

Chinese cards. I don't know if I told you or not, but I bought a deck as a souvenir, and then asked one of the Chinese here to teach me to use them. We had a good time and I've learned to play two of their games but am learning a more complicated one now.

There are 84 cards in the deck. There are no suits. The cards are made up similar to any roll of a pair of dice. Thus, there are 21 possible combinations on the dice and there are 4 cards for each one of those combinations. Thus, we have 3 different kinds of 6, 7, 8, two of other numbers, and only one of other numbers. It's quite interesting, but more later.

November 27, 1944

Although China is not quite as bleak as the picture Dragon Seed would have you suppose, Hollywood has turned out a pretty good Chinese setting. As I say, somehow they seem to give the scenery a parched, dry look in spite of the rice paddies. This is exactly the impression I always had of China until I came here. In reality, it is quite green, and green all through the year, with lovely sunshiny days, crispy nights, with tangerines and oranges the crop of the moment, while water buffalo pull the plows to break ground for the winter wheat. It's a Ding How country. Inflation is tremendous here, one dollar buying anywhere from $500 to $600. At this rate of exchange, a $10 bill is worth but 2¢. It's like a stock market, the exchange is so erratic. Of course, I always buy at the wrong time. (Like my horse race handicapping -- Boo How, or for variation -- Ya Boo Day (which means the same thing).

INDIA - December 10, 1944

This is truly the land of sunshine, quite a change from the weather we were experiencing on the other side of the hump. It's comparable to a winter trip to Miami, with warm days and cool nights. Everything looks the same as it used to dry and baked, and dirty. The people still run around in sheets and are as black as they were before. However, there's a certain niceness about it all, the brick-red soil, the brown grass, and the scraggly trees, in all its aridness.

It certainly was fine to get back and visit with old friends that I hadn't seen for seven months. The beer situation being good down here, we gather in the N.2.0. Club (a very nice one) around the foaming glasses and go over old times. Then there is the ice cream which just isn't t'other side of the hump.

And speaking about the hump, we got a very fine view of it this time and I managed to take a few pictures. The last time we flew over it was overcast, and we saw practically nothing. This time there were always peep holes in the clouds to view through. That certainly is a rock-pile! Some parts are green, some white, most of it jagged and rough. We went to a little town near here and took some snapshots. Although it was quite dirty, it was interesting, and we had to hitch-hike 15 miles to get there. We ate at a British Canteen and watched the oh! so typical Britishers bowling on the green -- "Nice shot, Bailey old boy!" -- and all that sort of thing, don't you know? This is just a note. More later about more happenings.

December 17, 1944

Since my last letter to you. I've visited Calcutta and had quite an enjoyable time. We spent (censored) sightseeing, eating, dining, and wining, having a wonderful time in a large old city. It felt good to be on our own and to vacation a bit, and we saw all that we could in the time allotted us. First of all, Calcutta is a large and fairly modern city, and yet the new mingles with the old wherever one goes. Although they have street cars and double-decker buses, the same street will be taken up with buffalo carts, rickshaws, and gharrys (horse-drawn carriages). Their taxis (old autos brightly painted, and with bulb horns that squeeze out warning grunts) with a huge Sikh, full beard, turban and all, behind the wheel, remind me of an American Indian in full feather driving along in a limousine. (Do you get the picture?) And so it is with the people -- women in native dress, some with veils, men with turbans, Anglo-Indians in new world costume, English men and women, Chinese and many soldiers, all intermingled, so that you see a correctly attired Anthony Eden, passing a bed sheeted Mahatma, a pretty English girl passing a beggar woman, an army officer passing a native with a bundle the size of the Taj Mahal on his head.

But what did we visit? Well, there was the Jain Temple, the Sikh Temple, the Kali Temple, the Mohammedan Mosque, some burning Ghats. The marble palace (where Queen Victoria stayed when she was crowned Empress of India), the Zoo, Botanical Garden, Victoria Memorial, New Market, Great Banyan Tree, several department stores, all kinds of restaurants, the Black Hole of Calcutta, St. John's

Church -- well -- pretty much of the city -- using taxi, gharry and boat.

And so I climbed a minaret, shuffled around temples in stockinged feet peering at queer gods and listening to fantastic beliefs, such as worshiping monkeys, cow's feet, sacrificing goats (saw one that had been sacrificed), etc., saw temples that house all kinds of creeds, saw bodies burned, their ashes thrown into the sacred water of the Ganges, the relatives of the dead bathing in the same. Some of the temples were beautifully inlaid with silver, turquoise, tiles of color, and glittered like a gingerbread house in the sun. Inside this particular temple of mosaic, mirrors, marble, and silver (Jain Temple), in the center of the room under a fancy canopy, and surrounded by sparkle and luster, stood this tiny golden idol some 9-inches tall. A Jain priest was in the process of bathing it, pouring myrrh, and then water, brushing it carefully in a regular ritual, canting all the while, while incense burned, and a gong sounded loudly.

This Jain Temple was situated in an area disposed to temples of all different religions, and this area was laid out in a pattern of marble walks, fishponds, lattice and iron work and buildings just out of this world. It was more like a lavish exhibit at the World's Fair. One fish pool was entirely covered over with a thick green growth, purposely so, for their particular religion avoids killing anything, even ants, and lest the birds devour the fish, the pool has been covered this way for 40 years. (P.S. How do they know there are any fish in there?) I tell you, it was like a fairyland, and if Alice in Wonderland were to pop up suddenly with her queer looking cohorts, I wouldn't have been a bit surprised!

We took a ferry down-river past several burning Ghats to the Botanical Gardens, the most beautiful bit of greenery I've ever seen. There are no flowers there, just trees and lawn, more like a natural wood that has been raked up and taken care of. Palm trees are plentiful and little ponds are everywhere. Here, the Great Banyan Tree, with the branches that sprout roots and spread, measures 1,152 feet in circumference around the foliage. The main trunk has rotted and has been chopped away, but the tree remains, a forest in itself. For the eating end, we visited the most fashionable hotels in town, and ate in a different place each time, having our fill of everything from steak to ice cream. And so, here I am in the warm Miami weather of India, basking in the early morning sunlight, and telling you about a strange country.

CHINA - December 26, 1944

Merry Christmas to you from my base back in dear old China. I got back for the holidays, and all in all we had quite a pleasant Christmas, the Chinese doing their best to make it as merry as possible. To start off, we had midnight services at the Red Cross Club. A Chinese priest said mass, one who said he had been a devout Buddhist till he was 19 years old, went to mass one day, saw how he was as welcome as anyone, (at that time the Chinese were not always thought equal), thought that there might be something in a religion that fostered this, looked into the matter, and in three years became a monk.

The next morning, Christmas, went rapidly, what with sleeping late, doing a bit of work, and then cleaning up and dressing for dinner (for the first time in a year). The Chinese spent a lot of time decorating the mess hall with Christmas trees, evergreens, paper Santa's, bells, etc., and at one end of it they had made a huge cake about 3-feet high, all decorated with dragons and the like in white and colored sugar. The meal was very good, the turkey coming from the States (in cans). Then came the cigar smoking period, and then a walk along the river, a light supper, and then free beer, free whiskey at the officers' club, fireworks, and a grand old time.

I'll tell you more about the fireworks which we also had on Christmas eve. One was donated to us by the Chinese General in this area (he visited us on Christmas) and the other was from the little town near here, given to us by the mayor. (Another town sent a huge cake). Their fireworks are in the form of a pageant and tell a story. They hoist a box (hexagonally shaped) and everything is contained in that box. A long streamer of firecrackers and fountains and rockets is attached at the bottom. This is lit and the performance begins with a clatter, in a shower of sparks. When the string of fireworks burns up to the box, suddenly four lanterns fall out and hang around the edges and light up and burn throughout the entire performance. Then suddenly down comes the first display, maybe a display with Chiang Kai Shek's picture on it and "Long Live Chiang" written on it. Of course, all this is lit up inside and flares are continually going off, together with all kinds of fountains, etc. (All these displays are made of tissue paper painted up and pasted around a very light frame of bamboo splints and fold up inside the box). Well, they have a number of displays of Chinese figures, etc., all symbolic of something. One was of an American bomber with 4 Jap planes overhead. One by one the Jap planes exploded in mid-air and vanished. (When one display is over it drops off and another falls out. The whole thing is worked by a continuous fuse). Another was of a Chinese and a Jap. The Chinese is holding a huge pistol and shoots the Jap who topples over backwards in a loud explosion. So, you see, we had quite a nice time, and have enough beer left over for several parties. Of course, New Year is coming.

30 January 25, 1945

Being on C.Q tonight, and thus having use of a typewriter, I thought I would hunt and peck on same as a diversion and write to you at the same time, thus hitting two birds with one rock. China is still China and it still strikes my fancy pretty well. The other day I did a little more local exploration, took off in an opposite of the usual direction, walked through some strange little towns and saw some new and interesting things. Coming to a sampan-laden river, I crossed it at an old mill where the sluiceways guided the water over horizontal wheels that turned a shaft that ran up through the floor of the mill which hung out over the stream. Inside (the Chinese miller invited me in and showed me around), were the millstones grinding out some kind of little round brown seed into a tan damp flour. My guide then led me to the next phase of operations in back of the mill where they heated the flour over brick ovens and compressed it into circular discs as hard as oak, to be used for what I could not understand in spite of a pantomimed explanation by my humble Chinese friend. I could only "Boo Doong"and wonder. Later, however, I saw some stacked in a restaurant and presume them to be used for making this Chinese sauce.

It's such a different country to behold, the landscape of rice paddies, bamboo and cedar, and burial mounds having a certain fascination and beauty, and the dusty walled alleyways of the towns, the strong stone bridges with their decoration of dragons spanning the rivers, the simple small plain-clothed people in their long dresses and silly hats, all combining to give an atmosphere that reeks with originality and strangeness. From the foregoing, I guess you are convinced that I like China, and that I am a very poor typist. Well, the darn magic margin has lost its mystic powers as you can see by the ragged leading edge, China has lost none of it!

INDIA - January 28, 1945

From your recent letter I gather that you probably will be glad to know that I am back in India again. You seemed concerned about the "dangers" of China. Anyway, now your minds can rest easy, for its peaceful Miami Beach days again. Yes, it was over the hump again, this time bucking a 90-mile-an-hour headwind. That certainly is rugged, beautiful country down there, but rough! And here we are, basking in this tropic sunshine, quite a change in climate. I pulled a fast strip act when the plane landed, getting rid of a sheep-lined jacket, a sweater, and a wool undershirt in a hurry.

You also refer to the old moustache. Well, it was getting in the way, I admit, so when I landed one of the first things accomplished was to -- trim it! (Bet you thought I'd say shave it off!) No! I just cut about an inch from it, so it has no twirl anymore, but that's as far as I'll go till we get back to the States. After "Samson's" locks were shorn, and as S. was reclining in the barracks, the Major (our Commanding Officer) walked in, nodded, he looked sharply at him, said "Is that you, Fisher," and after S. convinced him that it was, the Major came back with "What did you do with your moustache" in a rather disappointed and scolding voice. So, you can see what it would mean to take the whole thing off! No one would know me, and the Major could no longer point me out as the wearer of a set of handlebars!

February 2, 1945

Back from Calcutta again where we had a good time just wandering. I've told you all about it in the enclosure. So, India is dirty and full of disease, is it? Well, of course, it isn't as clean as it is out on Long Island, but one gets used to the dirt and sees very little disease. First impressions are bad, and the little towns are filthy, but one gets used to even these, and it's fun just to wander through them and see how the people live. The little Chinese towns are pretty dirty, too, and so you see we are used to it and it doesn't bother us at all. Of course, the camp is very clean. I would much rather be in China, though, for it is a much nicer country all around.

The Bombay Mail clattered into Howrah Station, across the river Hooghly from Calcutta and deposited us along with a mixture of black and white companions, into a jam at the taxi stand, as black boys tried to pull taxis out of the thin air (like their fakir forebears) to accommodate everyone at once, and their pockets in particular, at the rate of two annas a cab. Finally, we succeeded in getting a Sikh-jockeyed taxi and honked our way over Howrah Bridge and through jams of buffalo carts, gharries (horse driven carriages), people, and herds of cattle and goats, by ghats and stalls, temples, and halls, to the center of teeming Calcutta. Everything was as we had left it a month ago, and it wasn't long before we had secured lodging and were on our own in the second largest city in the British Empire.

It's too bad that the war has come to Calcutta, as it has to so many cities, for army installations have occupied much of its park space, crowding its pre-war spaciousness. Protection is everywhere in the form of walls of brick erected to protect civilian shops, etc., and necessary I expect, for the city was raided as recently as Christmas night of '44. Dimouts are necessary at night, too, giving it a difference and mysteriousness that wasn't there before. But what was there for us to visit? We had seen the famous Jain Temple, and many others, had been up the river, visited burning ghats, gardens, palaces, parks, zoos, and fashionable eating places, on our previous visit. True, we had some shopping to do -- the rest of the time was left to absorb atmosphere in the by-ways and "off limit"" surroundings of the city. The extensiveness of our shopping precluded the use of cabs, and so we took to riding trolleys, and reveled in beating the conductor out of his one anna and five pice fare. The method employed is the running mount, the only requirements a fair wind and a stout pair of legs.

The cars are hooked in pairs, the entrance has no doors that open and close, but a wide step for the convenience of boarding and disembarking on the gallop. Talk about subway rushes! They hang on that step by mysticism alone! The fares are figured out just as mysteriously, in pieces, which are made up of 4 pice to the anna and 16 annas to the rupee, catch? No? Well, neither do I. You just hand him two annas and hope you get back an anna and a coupon, good for one pice -- oh! well -- anyway, now that you understand that, we'll leave the streetcar (on the dead run, of course) and visit the Bow Bazaar (or Thieves' Market), strictly "off limits" to troops, of course. (The army always manages to put the most interesting spots on the blacklist -- the GI always manages to see them anyway).

The market got its crooked name honestly, for it's nothing more than a second-hand market where thieves got rid of their loot in former days (and probably still do). It's nothing but a series of stalls lining both sides of the alleys that squeeze themselves tortuously around crowds of humanity, stalls offering dusty wares amidst filth, hubbub, and the smell of fish. We drifted through with the crowds, wandered on into another alley of markets, vegetables, fruits, and fish being offered for sale, and so into another until the size reduced itself to a matter of will-I-make-it-or-will-I-not. We decided not to try, so took to wandering the streets, stopping at restaurants, (not recognizable by this name), cloth stores, jewelry manufacturers, etc., curious to see how everything was done. And so, our steps took us up a short alley, wherein was a shop, on the porch of which a native was intently busy at some native craft, no doubt. But lo! doesn't that look like machinery? And then we realize that he's rewinding a generator as he pauses, looks up, and says in perfect English, "I'm replacing the commutator!" So much for the native quarter.

Calcutta at night is another experience in itself. Sound takes over where sight leaves off, and through the dimness, as the cars creep and feel their way through the streets with very dim headlights to guide them, as people stumble along by the meager glow of candles being burned by the sidewalk peddlers, one hears the throaty honk of the quaint bulb horns of the taxis, the melodic scale of a boy selling flutes, the "Baksheesh, Sahib" of the beggar woman together with the sight of her with the usual child, the ever-present outstretched palm, the clang of the trolleys, perhaps the soothing words of a song crooned Eastern style by a troubadour on a slithering bicycle, the dull clunk of the bells of the rickshaw boys, the "Shine, Joe" of the shoeshine kids, the soft pimpy whisper "Nice white girls, Sahib," the "Hut" the gharry drivers to their stumbling horses, the click of the horses' feet -- these are the noises to guide you in the absence of light.

But one needs more experience than mine to find himself about, for after circling in abandon through back alleys and dark streets for an hour in search of my living quarters, I fell upon the mercy of a rickshaw wallah, who ferried me in the opposite direction two blocks and deposited me at my doorstep!

Now, back to the native quarter, this time down by the river, where we unsuccessfully hunted a ferry that would take us upstream for some riverfront sightseeing. Notice the bathing ghats directly downstream from the burning ghats, the 'female' ghat being separated from the male by 100 feet of open space and a loin cloth. What muddy water to bathe in (not the 'clean' yellowish mud of the Mississippi, but the greyish-brown mud of stagnation) no less to drink from as that man just did, while his partner anoints himself with oil.

As we pass Nimtala burning ghat we see through the entrance several attendants arranging another Hindu, a cold one, on his mango-wood funeral pyre. One can see 'holy men' about. There is a fire worshiper as evidenced by the coating of ash with which he has powdered himself from head to loin cloth to feet, and by the cow dung in his hair. Although he's standing in front of a food stall at present, he will soon again be before his fire, gazing into it, gesticulating, mumbling, and spreading ashes over himself. There is another 'holy man' -- I don't know what he worships but his forehead is painted white and red, and he wears a string of bones about his neck and suspended from his waist dangle two glossy white skulls.

But let us pass on away from the waterfront up the narrow alleys and winding streets, pausing long enough to let a funeral procession pass by. Very simple it is, too. Four pallbearers, with a rope bed on which lies a figure draped to the chin in a sheet, with flower leis carelessly thrown atop, proceed toward the burning ghat we have just left. (Quite different from the Chinese funeral we saw on the previous day in the streets proper of Calcutta, and so often in China, the casket headed by a parade of white bedecked mourners, a brass band, and flying flags and banners.)

I want to show you a little about eating here in Bengal.

Rice and flour (wile) are their staples, of course, but to stop in front of a food stall is to gaze at odd-shaped, peculiar fried things and wonder how these edibles are prepared. Most of them fried in deep fat in big iron pots that are shaped hemispherically and have two handles. Take one kind, for instance, a pretzelly looking thing made of some kind of white flour. The mixture is about the consistency of pancake batter and is poured into half a coconut shell, suspended over the pot of hot fat, and allowed to pour through a hole in the bottom of the shell by the simple means of the man removing his finger from the hole. He pours it in never-ending spirals until the pot is full of a bubbly endless pretzel. It cooks up crisp and looks tasty, but we didn't try one. Then they have something similar to tortillas, but a bit more puffy. One of the most unusual sights, though, is to watch them bake big round doughy cakes that resemble a pizza shell without the filling. This is done in an open oven. The dough is made into a rubbery ball, twirled until it is flat and round, then placed over a round pillow and slammed up against the clay wall on the inside of the oven, where it sticks (like the slabs of cow dung on the walls of any home) and cooks rapidly. A long rod with a hook on it is used with great dexterity to twirl the cake off the wall and up through the open hole of the oven. A good crew of men working fast can really turn out the cakes. But our pass is nearly over. We have barely enough time to get to the station and board the Madras Mail. So long, Calcutta, and may we visit you another time.

February 15, 1945

I did forget to tell you about the snake charmers, with whom India is so closely associated. They carry their snakes in two bags slung at the ends of a pole across their shoulders. They will play their pipes to a gyrating cobra for the usual silver. The fakir (should be faker) I saw was letting his pet snake strike at him playfully, the best of friends, the snake probably signed up to a long-term contract, and toothless with old age. But the cobra was incidental to the snakes he started to produce by the yard from his two bundles. In went his hand, out came another, all shapes, sizes and colors -- one bright green, one 6-feet long, another quite heavy of body and marked like a python, probably a baby one, and so on until the ground around him was alive with them, some with ideas of their own who tried to take it on the duffy through the crowd. The payoff was when the old fakir grabbed a tin can and dumped out a wriggling mass into his hand, proffered them to us with the words, "nice fresh scorpions!"

I also forgot to tell you about the dairy situated in the corner of a smelly open-air market. Each one with milk to sell had his pail sitting in front of him in the hot sun, open to flies, and with straw floating around the edges to keep it from spilling in transit. A prospective customer approaches to purchase a can full. Now which milk will he choose? How does he know which is watered the most? Easy! He dips his hand into them and lets the milk run between his fingers!

We went to the ballet while in town, the first to perform in Calcutta since 1935. "Twas from London. Of course, it didn't compare to the Ballet Russe, although one little lady quite caught my fancy. She was really good. Reminded me of someone mixed in with a dash of someone else, if you get what I mean. Anyway, it was too bad we were to go home that afternoon, or I would have seen the show on the morrow.

February 16, 1945

I got a great laugh out of Willets, one of the boys with me on a recent trek into the mountains. There we were in the middle of the mountains, on foot and stranded thirty miles from nowhere, trudging along, and he had his nose in Ripley's Believe It or Not, reading all about the strange land of India. I didn't tell you about that trip, did I? Well, Willets, Mike Warranch and I went hitchhiking to a town 110 miles from here and stayed overnight, got stranded on the way back, and luckily were saved a thirty-mile walk (we already had hiked ten) through the mountains by getting a ride on a gook (native) coal and delivery truck. (That word '"gook"- rhymes with spook - is a GI nickname given to the Indians. We happened to be speaking to a British Major one day, used this GI reference, he didn't catch on, so we translated for him, then asked if they had a nickname for them. He was a typical Britisher, all officer, tall, lanky, big long face, in silly shorts, of course, and he answered in his best accent, very British you know, that they called them "Wogs"- rhymes with frogs -- and translated thus, "Wily Oriental Gentleman, y'know!")

The trip was just a breather, a sort of respite from idleness. We got itchy feet and just took off. Saw quite a bit too, steel mills, mines, nice mountains, quite a nice town, had some wild rides along mountain roads (the wildest of many wild rides since I've been in the army). By the way, we're allowed to wear four battle stars on our Pacific theatre ribbon, one for India-Burma theatre, one for China, one for bombing Japan, and one for bombing Palambang in the East Indies.

Feel guilty -- so much for so little.

Sergeant Edward Southworth Fisher
US Army Air Corps (approx. 1942)

A Competition was held by the U.S. Mint for the selection
of a commemorative coin for the 1991-1995
50th Anniversary of World War II.
Ed Fisher's design was chosen for the reverse side of the
Gold Five-Dollar coin depicted above.
His initials ESF can be seen in the lower left section.

Made in the USA
Middletown, DE
29 September 2020